'Death: the great common deno
taboo. How do young people ur
it? How does it "work" in the w
each other and to themselves? How does it shape or
their ambitions and their sense of justice? Immensely
readable, full of wisdom, and enriched by vivid case material,
Nick Luxmoore's book provides answers to these questions.
It will be invaluable reading for anyone working with young
people.'

– Ron Best, Emeritus Professor of Education,
University of Roehampton

'Nick Luxmoore is one of the outstanding writers on the
adolescent stage of life. He tackles issues and asks questions
that, for most of us, are too hot to handle. In this book he
encourages us to think the unthinkable, that teenagers are
concerned with death and with their own mortality. This is
a fascinating and important book, and should be read by all
who are concerned with the lives, particularly the inner lives,
of young people.'

– Dr John Coleman OBE, Senior Research
Fellow, University of Oxford

'The book is a useful read for helping professionals and
parents. The nuances of severe adolescent grief and suffering
are effectively discussed. The narrative is real-world and
compelling, not sugar-coated as some books are when
addressing the complex issues of death and existential pain.'

– Christopher Sink, PhD, Professor of Counselor
Education at Seattle Pacific University and Editor
of the Professional School Counseling Journal

YOUNG PEOPLE, DEATH AND THE UNFAIRNESS OF EVERYTHING

NICK LUXMOORE

Jessica Kingsley *Publishers*
London and Philadelphia

LA MORT Words and Music by Jacques Brel © 1967 Editions Poucherel Musicales. All Rights Reserved. Lyric reproduction by kind permission of Carlin Music Corporation, London NW1 8BD.

First published in 2012
by Jessica Kingsley Publishers
116 Pentonville Road
London N1 9JB, UK
and
400 Market Street, Suite 400
Philadelphia, PA 19106, USA

www.jkp.com

Library of Congress Cataloging in Publication Data
Luxmoore, Nick, 1956-
   Young people, death, and the unfairness of everything / Nick Luxmoore.
      p. cm.
   Includes bibliographical references and index.
   ISBN 978-1-84905-320-4 (alk. paper)
   1. Teenagers and death. 2. Children and death. 3. Bereavement in adolescence. 4. Bereavement in
children. 5. Grief in adolescence. 6. Grief in children. I. Title.
   BF724.3.D43L89 2012
   155.9'37083--dc23
                          2012007707

British Library Cataloguing in Publication Data
A CIP catalogue record for this book is available from the British Library

ISBN 978 1 84905 320 4
eISBN 978 0 85700 662 2

Printed and bound in Great Britain

For
David Buckland

La mort m'attend comme une
princesse
A l'enterrement de ma jeunesse

FROM 'LA MORT' BY JACQUES BREL

CONTENTS

ACKNOWLEDGEMENTS

I'm grateful to Carlin Music Corporation for permission to quote from 'La Mort' by Jacques Brel.

I'm also grateful to colleagues at King Alfred's College, Wantage, for supporting my work, especially to Simon Spiers, Adam Arnell, Kate Baker and Diane Jones. I'm grateful to my supervisor, Jane Campbell, and to Kathy Peto, Ben Reed-Berendt, Debbie Lee, Professor Chris Mowles and Jane Campbell for reading and commenting on drafts of this book. Big thankyous, as ever, to Kathy, Frances and Julia.

1

INTRODUCTION

In bright sunshine young people are leaping to catch basketballs or they're indoors peering at laboratory experiments through protective glasses. They're illuminated on stage in costumed productions or fooling around in fancy dress for charity. Sometimes they're crouched over desks in an examination hall or they're abroad somewhere, posing in front of a famous landmark.

School prospectuses are adorned with images like these of young people absorbed in worthwhile educational activities. It's how we like to think of the young people we love: by creating these opportunities, we've put smiles on their faces, we've instilled in them a zest for life and sense of achievement. Prospectuses can't show pictures of young people looking disconsolate or angry or afraid: that would spoil things and no parent would want to send their son or daughter to that school!

The problem isn't school prospectuses. They have a job to do and that job isn't to create more emotionally honest societies. School prospectuses are only symptomatic of our more general reluctance to engage with the flip-side of all those happy faces – with young people's doubting, questioning, wondering about what it's all for and, at the sharp end of that wondering, with their anxiety about what happens at the end of everything. 'Death's the last thing on their minds,' we tell each other. 'They've got their whole lives ahead of them. Why would they want to be thinking about death? That's morbid! They'll worry about that when they're much older.'

Nursing our own anxieties about death, this may be what we'd *like* to believe, but it's not true. As this book describes, young people worry about death and dying and about the meaning of their own eventual non-existence far more than is popularly supposed. This isn't a book about working with terminally ill young people. Rather, it's about trying to understand and help young people who may well live to be a hundred but who – in all sorts of conscious and unconscious ways – are anxious about death and dying, about why things happen and about the point of anything. In a sense, all young people are 'terminal'; they're only too well aware of the fact and they end up *enacting* their anxieties for lack of opportunities to talk about them.

Wherever they look, young people are shielded from death and encouraged to think about other things. Euphemisms abound: nowadays we 'pass away' or 'fall asleep' or are simply 'lost', as if to 'die' would be somehow rude. Deaths are habitually described as 'tragic' rather than inevitable. We have health and safety policies trying to anticipate every eventuality, while we're distanced from the physicality of death by hospitals and undertakers whose energies go into sanitising the whole business as much as possible.

Worrying about death, we worry about ageing. We talk scornfully of people 'letting themselves go' as if to age visibly were somehow shameful and defeatist with so many age-defying products available in the shops. We put off making our wills. We plan for a long retirement. 'Our disbelief in death grows in proportion to its approach,' writes Koestler (quoted in Barnes 2008, p.137). And if death does come, despite our best attempts to pretend otherwise, then surely it must have been someone's fault? Surely more could have been done? Surely someone at the hospital must have made a mistake? It's as if we've discarded our religious fantasies of immortality only to replace them with medical and technological fantasies. Somehow the doctors will keep us alive. Somehow they'll prevent us from suffering. Davies (2012) describes how our understanding of suffering has changed dramatically over the centuries. Where suffering was once seen as noble, enlightening and redemptive, nowadays we regard it as unfair, punitive and avoidable. Where suffering was once regarded as a profoundly humanising experience, nowadays we look to the pharmaceutical industry to liberate us from any kind of discomfort.

We end up believing that we have a right to be free from suffering, a right to be happy and a right to be in control of our lives. We look to education to give us these things: control over our environments, instincts and emotions; control over our despair and confusion. Children and young people, in particular, are expected to be happy, living up to the promises of the prospectus, yet '…happiness as a moral demand – you must be happy, and you are failing if you are not – is pernicious,' writes Phillips (2010, p.93). I work as a counsellor in a secondary school where, understandably, our institutional rhetoric is all about the future, the future, the future with its promises of happiness and control. Our rhetoric is never about what happens at the end of all the exciting futures that we're proposing for young people. And yet so much of what those young people bring to my counselling room relates directly and indirectly to their existential anxieties and, in particular, to their anxieties about death – the very thing that they're not supposed to be worrying about.

Adults readily project their own sense of unfulfilled potential onto young people (Luxmoore 2008) and it's this sense of unfulfilled potential that makes young people so maddening. 'You've got your whole life ahead of you! You've got to make the most of it! You could do anything!' Hearing this, young people are left with an idealised sense of how they're supposed to be. Inevitably they fail to live up to the idealisation, wasting time, making mistakes, prevaricating, saying that they don't care. And so, once they're failing, various experiences are prescribed to shock them into action: a dose of work experience to make them realise what the real world is like; a few days' exclusion to bring them to their senses; a spell in prison to teach them that this behaviour won't be tolerated... All these prescriptions obliquely threaten young people with death because they're all experiences of being cast out, alone, unsupported and forced to confront some ultimate, chastening kind of reality. 'You've only got one life! How can you waste it?'

Death is threatened but never talked about explicitly. Because of this, young people grow up with a question mark hanging over them – a question mark that leaves them anxious, ungrounded, living a life where one kind of future is idealised and celebrated while the other is avoided, blocked out and dreaded. In one of these futures, they live for evermore; in the other, they die. Adults defend themselves against the prospect of death by idealising youthfulness, promoting and rewarding it even as they joke sardonically about getting older, greyer, fatter and stiffer themselves. They exaggerate their own remembered youth as if to revive it, comparing it endlessly with that of the young people they know today who seem so lucky and so infuriatingly unaware of their luck.

Young people claim not to understand what all the fuss is about: 'If you're going to die anyway, then what's the point of worrying?' But, secretly, they understand perfectly well and worry a lot. For hormonally excited bodies, everything is about growth and accumulation, but with physical excitements come psychological anxieties. What if, like Ozymandias in Shelley's poem, all our endeavours come to nothing? What if everything eventually falls down like the towers of bricks children build up and knock down, build up and knock down, delighting in their apparent omnipotence? What will it be like when the waves wash away the sandcastles and breakwaters we've spent so many hours making in the full knowledge that this is *exactly* what the waves will do once the tide comes in? Faced with these anxieties, young people's behaviour veers between grandiosity and despair, between 'Great! I'll live forever!' and 'Help! I could die at any moment!'

Writing about adolescence, Blos (1962) comments, 'The realization of the finality of the end of childhood, of the binding nature of commitments, of the definite limitation to individual existence itself – this realization creates a sense of urgency, fear, and panic' (p.12). Young people feel this urgency, fear and panic even as they're being envied for their youthfulness and encouraged not to think about death for fear of contaminating the images in the prospectus. As with some dreadful political scandal, the adult cover-up gets desperate because the stakes are so high. We know that death will get the better of us one day, despite all our wealth and achievements, our excellent medical insurance. But perhaps our children will be spared? Perhaps their lives will be free from death and from the threat of death, from the anxieties that preoccupy us as parents and as professionals?

In Thomas Mann's (1912, 1973) novella *Death in Venice*, a successful but ageing writer falls in love with a fourteen-year-old boy who seems to have a 'godlike beauty', to be a 'masterpiece from nature's own hand'. The writer gazes endlessly at the boy, admiring his youth and beauty. He supposes that one day the boy will die like everyone else and yet there seems to be something 'eternal' about his beauty which, like a work of art, ought to survive physical death. Aware of his own mortality and wishing that his own art could be immortal, the writer curses, 'What good can an artist be as a teacher, when from his birth he is headed direct for the pit? We may want to shun it and attain to honour in the world; but however we turn, it draws us still' (p.81). Ironically, in the beautiful city of Venice, where so many great works of art are preserved, death is everywhere, a plague of cholera creeping up on the city's inhabitants. Realising that his own death is inescapable, the writer can only lament the fact that the boy's youth and beauty must also die.

The thought of the happy, smiling young people in the prospectus actually dying one day is so unbearable that we won't talk with them about it. And yet it's when the pressure *not* to think about death is greatest that young people's underlying anxieties about death are also greatest and most likely to seep out or explode in ways I'll describe in later chapters.

I remember my first day as a counsellor with young asylum seekers and refugees. I had a pile of induction reading in front of me and included in that reading was a large, yellow book containing the testimonies of people who'd survived the Rwandan genocide. I was curious as I began to read these first-hand accounts, but the more I read, the more predictable it became – page after page of horror – until I found myself laughing. Not laughing like when you watch a funny film but laughing with incredulity; laughing because I couldn't make the empathic leap required to imagine the extent of the suffering and terror recorded in this book; laughing to protect myself; laughing to stay sane, probably as the killers laughed, going about their business: laughing to survive.

We can't help defending ourselves against the prospect of death. The problem comes when we defend young people on behalf of ourselves, depriving them of opportunities to think and talk about death with another person rather than always having to think about death on their own. By encouraging young people not to think about death, we deprive them of opportunities to develop their own defences, which are likely to be less bizarre and self-destructive if young people have had opportunities to think about death calmly, regularly and with the support of people unafraid to join them in their thinking (Adams 2010). This book describes ways of trying to respond openly to young people's concerns without shutting down their thinking or trying to shape their wondering in any particular way, religious or otherwise.

At the age of about six, most children go through a phase of asking their parents about death... 'Why do people die, Mum? What happens to people when they die, Dad? Will you die? What will happen to me if you die?' To these questions they receive all sorts of answers – some scientific, some religious, some that have nothing whatsoever to do with the question and some that are intended to be comforting but end up sounding completely bizarre.

'I was told that Mum and Dad would be waiting for me in heaven,' remembers Thalassa, 'and there'd be a party and everyone I'd ever known would be there. But I got scared because I didn't want to meet Neville Jones in heaven. He used to bully me!'

Dag was told that his body would rot in the ground but – not to worry – he wouldn't feel a thing because he wouldn't be there. 'So I asked where I'd be and my dad said I'd be in a better place. When I asked what sort of place, he laughed and said he didn't know because he hadn't been there!'

If, as Blos (1962) claims, adolescence is a recapitulation of childhood, with young people reworking an original set of issues and dilemmas, then how do sixteen-year-olds rework the questions they once asked as six-year-olds? It feels childish still to be asking the same questions, so how *do* young people re-engage adults on the subject of death?

The answer is that they don't. Not for lack of curiosity but because they've long since picked up the message: it's a taboo subject; it's not what we talk about; talking about death might upset someone. It's genuinely hard for parents to know what to say in any case – wanting to allay their children's fears whilst feeling that, as parents, they should have the answers to such important questions. Yalom (1980) writes that 'Generally parents attempt to assuage a child's fears by offering some form of denial, either some idiosyncratic denial system or a socially sanctioned immortality myth' (p.82). It's assumed that the issue of death goes away once a six-year-old stops asking, but it doesn't. Fairytales may end with everyone living happily ever after… But until what? Until they have a heart attack? Until they get cancer, have chemotherapy and die? Until they have a fall, break a hip and never recover? Until they're stricken with Alzheimer's? The fairytale never ends with the death of the prince and princess although, along the way, plenty of *other* people will have been poisoned, eaten alive or killed in hideous ways. Children put down their fairytales and watch the news on television, full of people around the world dying or in danger of dying, sometimes dying in vast numbers. Women weep. Men scream vengeance. Bodies are carried through the streets. But it's always happening to other people and somewhere else in the world. We turn the television off, give generously and carry on with our lives.

Young people go back to their bedrooms and carry on with their computer games, many of which hinge on a struggle for survival. 'I was killed thirty-six times in ten minutes!' says Jordan excitedly, telling me about his latest game. Commentators may worry about young people's exposure to so much grisly killing, but I wonder whether violent computer games are less about the excitement of fighting and more about the fear of dying. I wonder whether young people obsessively explore issues about death through game-playing for lack of opportunities to explore death through talking. I wonder whether we'd have fewer mental health difficulties if we had a more robust approach to the idea of death, as in countries where death is all around and where young people grow up accustomed to seeing bodies laid out in the next room. Erikson (1950) writes, 'Healthy children will not fear life if their elders have integrity enough not to fear death' (p.269).

Of course, death isn't the *only* thing that young people worry about, nor is it the only thing affecting their behaviour. They have plenty of other concerns and they have happy experiences as well as difficult ones. But in my experience of young people, death is the subject that's always avoided and therefore becomes hardest to talk about – harder even than sex. There's the fact of tangible, physical death with which young people have to engage whenever someone they know is dying (see Chapter 2), but there's also the constant *idea* of death. That's much more elusive, much harder to name and yet always there, dogging young people like the ghost of Hamlet's father insisting to his poor son, 'Remember me!' There's the 'death' which young people anticipate as a personal annihilation, like becoming invisible, like not mattering to anyone (see Chapter 5); there's the 'death' involved in all sorts of important losses (see Chapter 6) and even a certain kind of 'death' involved in sexual orgasm (see Chapter 7).

Yalom (1980) writes that 'The ultimate task of therapy...is to help patients reconstrue that which they cannot alter' (p.273). This means engaging with the fact that death can't be altered and with the fact that all our endeavours will ultimately come to an end. It means thinking together about what sense to make of this predicament (see Chapter 8). This isn't a book about *what* young people should eventually understand about death and non-existence but a book about encouraging them to wonder about these things openly and often. In advocating a more proactive, robust conversation about death, I'm not arguing for more religious assemblies in schools or for young people to be indoctrinated in received religious beliefs. Religion can be as defensive a way of (not) thinking about death as it can be a helpful way. Rather, I'm arguing for a wondering about life and death to be at the heart of schools and at the heart of the conversations adults might have with young people. Whatever they end up believing, young people should at least be allowed – indeed, should be encouraged – to think and talk openly about death because the effect of *not* doing so is pernicious and leads to all sorts of unhappy, anxious behaviours. Young people may well come to believe in established religious beliefs about death or they may come to believe, like Bertrand Russell

(1925, p.13), that '…when I die I shall rot, and nothing of my ego will survive…' Science and technology won't save them from death any more than will religion.

At the school where I work, members of staff come to see me for counselling usually because they've reached a point in their lives where the old certainties no longer seem so certain, where the ambitions they once pursued either have not been achieved or no longer seem so urgent. Whatever the presenting problem, these hard-working professionals are still trying to make sense of their lives. They may be young, searching for a partner and scared of what the future will hold. They may be middle-aged and wondering what to make of life now that their children need them less obviously and promotion at work is no longer a realistic or even desirable possibility. They may be nearing retirement and wondering what life will hold once the patterns of work are no longer in place. Whatever 'meaning' has encased their lives until now, something's changing. This might be true for any adult visiting a counsellor: the difference for adults working with young people is that they find themselves expected to instil in those young people ambitions, goals and a sense of purpose, even as their own are sometimes faltering.

Young people have seen the prospectus and are perfectly well aware that this is what their parents and teachers are trying to do. Yalom (1980) writes:

> The Western world has…insidiously adopted a world view that there is a 'point', an outcome of all one's endeavours. One strives for a goal. One's efforts must have some end point, just as a sermon has a moral and a story, a satisfying conclusion. Everything is in preparation for something else. (p.469)

Young people are aware of the material goals which are so important to so many adults. But although some cling blindly to the pre-packaged ideas propounded by an admired person or organisation, most young people are intent on discovering their own meaning: meaning that makes sense of their own experience. The meaning they evince depends on the autobiographical story they're telling. Depending on that story, they might conclude that 'the world is against me' or that 'mothers should love their children'. They might decide that friends can't be trusted, that babies always get attention, that sex makes you powerful, that money makes fathers happy, that things are more reliable than people, that fame makes you popular... These are meanings or interpretations of experience that simplify and, for the time being, appear to make sense of life. It's easier to believe that you either love *or* hate your parents, for example, than acknowledge the fact that you might both love *and* hate them.

My job as a counsellor is to explore these beliefs with a young person, wondering where a particular belief has come from and whether it still holds up now that the circumstances of the young person's life have changed. As young people get older, the old love-or-hate, good-or-bad, me-or-you, us-or-them simplicities rarely make sense because they make no allowance for mixed motives, genuine mistakes and accidental cock-ups (see Chapter 8).

'I know it felt like everyone was picking on you. But I wonder whether what happened might have been less personal than it felt at the time?'

'It certainly felt personal!'

'I know it did. But maybe things got messed up? Maybe people were trying their best but simply got it wrong?'

As far as death is concerned, young people choose from another range of simplifications to explain a real or anticipated death that no one has helped them to think through. They might end up telling themselves that death is to be feared or that death is a relief. They might choose to believe that death is a punishment, that death can somehow be avoided, that death is an honourable escape when life gets hard, that death is failure, that death is glory... Our conversations begin to unpick these simplicities, searching for the meaning *in* life rather than the meaning *of* life.

'I'd hate to die before I'm old.'

'Because?'

'I don't know. It just wouldn't seem right, would it? You're supposed to die when you're old. Not when you're young... I hate it when they show programmes about kids with cancer.'

'Because of imagining what it would be like if you had cancer?'

'Yeah. And you see these kids dying when they've done nothing wrong and you think about all the bad things you've done in your life.'

'And you end up feeling guilty?'

'Yeah! Like, they're going to die but you've still got your whole life... Do you believe in reincarnation?'

In the film *Stand by Me* (Reiner 1986), four boys set out on a journey to find the body of a local boy, reputedly killed by a train within a day's walk of where they live. Each boy carries with him a troubled family history (death, bullying, alcoholism, violence) and along the way they have to deal with a gang of older boys – loud show-offs equally determined to find the body.

It's a wonderful film in which adults contribute absolutely nothing to the boys' experience. Instead, the boys embark on a journey from innocence to experience with no one to prepare or debrief them, their journey culminating in the macabre discovery of the body. Before its discovery, they share an excited curiosity about death. Having found it, they become private and alone, each boy deep in his own thoughts, cut off from the others. They return home sadder and wiser, deflated, the search for the body having put their own lives into sombre perspective. They go their separate ways and, according to the boy narrating, nothing is ever the same again.

Whenever young people go to see counsellors or other professionals, they're always asking, in effect, 'How exactly are you going to help me when everyone knows that the things that have happened in my life can't be changed?' or, by extension, 'Given that I'm going to die one day and you can't do anything about that, then what's the point of us talking?' The answer is that counsellors and other professionals can help us to live more peaceably, better able to bear the things we can't change. I sometimes interrupt young people who seem to be avoiding the subject and ask, 'Do you think much about death?' Always they engage with the question as if they've been waiting for it all along and I'm left thinking, 'What was I waiting for? Why didn't I ask sooner?'

This book is about supporting young people in their wondering about death. Julian Barnes (2008) paraphrases the philosopher Montaigne who believed that:

> …since we cannot defeat death, the best form of counter-attack is to have it constantly in mind: to think of death whenever your horse stumbles or a tile falls from a roof. You should have the taste of death in your mouth and its name on your tongue. To anticipate death in this way is to release yourself from its servitude: further, if you teach someone how to die, then you teach them how to live. (p.41)

2

THE PHYSICALITY OF DEATH

'Ay, but to die, and go we know not where;
To lie in cold obstruction and to rot...'

MEASURE FOR MEASURE III.1.118–19

Young people are scared of dying. Scared and intrigued.
'Will it hurt? Will I be missed? What'll happen to my
body? At what point will I be dead? Will I know if I'm
dead? What'll it be like to be dead?' They're curious about
their own imagined death and especially curious about
their funeral. 'Who'll be there? Who'll be crying? What'll
they be saying about me? Who'll be regretting all those
hurtful things they said? Who'll be realising – too late!
– what a wonderful person I was?' Like Hamlet holding
Yorick's skull in his hands and feeling sick, young people
experience the death of someone they know as scary but
also intriguing – seeing the coffin, imagining the person
inside it, imagining what will happen when the coffin is
taken away to be buried or cremated. In counselling, we
can wonder together about these thoughts and imaginings
because they're inevitable and because a conversation in
which they can be acknowledged as sensible (not silly) and
as interesting (not childish) is a relief for young people.

The scariness of death is partly because young people grow up with a clear message: death is evidently so frightening that adults refuse even to talk about it. But death is also intriguing: young people go into a museum and head straight for the mummies; they stay up all night on sleepovers watching horror films – zombies, cemeteries, rotting corpses. Yet when someone they know *actually* dies or is bereaved, all hell breaks loose. This is scary. This is uncharted territory and the rules are unclear. How should we behave? Should we cry hysterically or keep stoically silent? As I've written elsewhere (Luxmoore 2011), the dead person quickly becomes a saint in everyone's eyes and a posse is formed to protect the saint's reputation. Sooner or later, someone dares – perhaps unwittingly – to make a joke in bad taste or to question the saint's reputation, and the moral indignation of the posse is heaped upon the sinner. 'How could you say such a thing? About someone who's *dead*?' The dead person may be pitied but also becomes the object of everyone's envy because he or she is getting so much attention: admiring messages and tributes, masses of flowers, canonisation. In a way, it would be quite nice to be dead and get all that attention if it wasn't for the fact of having to die.

An observer might look cynically at young people's behaviour on these occasions. It's certainly stylised and everybody certainly has his or her own agenda, using the event to explore all sorts of issues which I'll describe in later chapters. This much may be true, but how else are young people supposed to behave when death has come to seem like such an unusual event? I've worked in schools where the death of anyone – a student, a teacher, a parent – is the cause of general panic (Luxmoore 2011) because the fact of death seems too much for 'ordinary' people to bear. 'What do I say? What if I say the wrong thing? What if someone cries?'

When someone dies, we need our *ordinary* relatives, friends and colleagues around us because death is *ordinary*. Of course, it's terribly sad and especially shocking when a young person dies, but, in a way, it's as ordinary as birth, as growing up, as getting old. It happens. We're all 'fastened to a dying animal', in Yeats's (1999) phrase. It's really important that young people are able to think and talk about death and dying without adults pretending that somehow none of us will ever die. Young people need to know the facts. They need to be allowed to react in their different ways which include pretending that nothing has happened. There are no standard or ideal responses.

Two of my most spectacular mistakes as a school counsellor have involved death. On the first occasion, I was working in a school where a student had stopped attending. We enquired and found out from his family that he was dying of a brain tumour. Before long, all the students in the school had found out as well and everyone was wondering what would happen next. Was he about to die? When would he die?

I met with senior staff and we agreed that, as soon as the boy died, we'd tell the whole school. We wanted everyone to know what was happening so that their experience of this death would be clear, honest and proportionate. We wouldn't flinch from the news, but life in school would carry on. The boy's death would be absorbed as part of everyone's experience: not euphemistically, not as if some impossible disaster had occurred, but in a way that we hoped would be emotionally healthy. This was an opportunity to teach young people something important about the inevitability of death.

A few weeks later, the boy's sister came into school one morning in tears and informed her teacher that her brother had died.

Immediately we put our plan into operation. A colleague and I visited every classroom, interrupting whatever was going on to inform every class that the boy had died. Within an hour, the whole school community knew and we were pleased that they'd heard the news from us in a way that was clear, respectful and not inflammatory.

Half an hour later, a teacher was commiserating with the boy's sister, saying how sorry he was to hear the news.

'Well,' said the girl, 'I *think* he's dead. When I left this morning, he hadn't said anything for ages!'

'Was he breathing?'

'I *think* he was breathing, yes...'

We had no alternative but to go round to every classroom again, explaining that, in fact, the boy *hadn't* died.

My second mistake happened when I was seeing a student for the first time. It was explained to me that his father had killed himself a few weeks earlier which was why the boy was upset in school and had agreed to see me.

Sometimes I meet with young people having already heard all sorts of things about them and so, if it seems appropriate, I begin by saying what I've heard. Young people know perfectly well that professionals talk to each other in private and that counsellors get told things. I didn't want this relationship to begin with elephants in the room or with the boy having fantasies about what I knew and didn't know. In particular, I didn't want his father's suicide to become something we couldn't name or speak about. I imagined his teachers avoiding the subject altogether for fear of getting it wrong. So, before inviting him to speak, I finished my preamble about counselling and confidentiality by adding, 'And the only thing I know about you already is that your father killed himself a few weeks ago...'

'He did?' The boy's eyes widened. 'Oh no! Oh *no!*'

I realised to my horror that no one had actually told him how his father had died. Nor had anyone told me that the boy didn't know.

I spent the rest of the session trying to recover some ground but, still reeling from what he'd been told and the way in which he'd been told it, the boy had no interest in making another appointment with me.

I cursed myself. But although the results were disastrous, I think my intention on both these occasions was right. If young people can talk explicitly about death, it becomes less frightening. Someone dying is a chance for young people to learn, to question and not be scared. In my experience, young people who have experienced the death of someone important seem better able to think about death and dying than those young people who, for one reason or another, have been shielded from death. However upsetting it may be at the time, the experience of someone they know dying actually helps young people in many ways.

A long time ago, I worked as a hospital porter where part of the job involved collecting dead bodies from the wards. We'd wheel our special trolley to the ward, lift the body onto it, close the lid and wheel the trolley away again down a succession of corridors to the mortuary. Once there, we'd find an empty shelf in one of the fridges, slide the body onto it, record what we'd done and go back to our porters' room.

This job was known to the porters as 'doing a carry-out', making it sound as if we were collecting a takeaway meal. I remember everyone laughing one day when a tearful junior nurse phoned the porters' room to tell us – very politely – that she had 'a patient to go to the mortuary'.

We all joined in. 'Ha! You mean a carry-out!'

In my first weeks of the job, I thought a lot about carry-outs – about the warmth sometimes of the body wrapped in a sheet flimsily held together with tape that was always likely to pull apart; about how small many of the bodies seemed; about the things we'd see as we opened the fridge doors, especially if it was during the daytime and the morticians were at work next door. I used to think about these things as I lay in bed at night, grimly trying to get to sleep. But after a few weeks in the job I got used to carry-outs and stopped thinking about them.

Only after I'd left the job did I start thinking about them again, and, again, they became scary. It was as if I could afford to let my guard down and think about the physicality of death only once I was no longer dealing every day with bodies and mortuaries. Whilst I was doing the job, I got on with it. I didn't think. I just did carry-outs, ha, ha!

Joey also has no choice but to get on with it. His father is dying at home. Joey seems relieved that I want to know all about his father's condition and he tells me the facts. A week later, I hear that his father has died and, some time after that, Joey comes back to school.

Hesitant at first, he tells me about what happened on the night his father died. He tells me about what happened during the days that followed and at the funeral. Unusually for a young person, he thanks me at the end of the session.

When we meet for the third time, there are plenty of recent happenings to discuss and we start to explore his feelings – in particular, his mixed feelings: sad but also relieved that his father is dead after such a long illness; loving his father but angry with him for getting ill and dying; wanting to remember his father but also wanting to go out and get drunk with friends. I'm impressed by Joey's honesty and he seems relieved to hear that mixed feelings like these are understandable to another person. He worries that he hasn't cried like his younger brother but, instead, has found himself getting angry over small things at home.

As the weeks and months go by, he worries about not visiting his father's grave. The rest of the family have been several times and haven't minded him not going, he says, but he feels guilty all the same.

It becomes a stumbling block. The more time passes, the harder it becomes to visit the grave. I think it reminds Joey of the physicality of death that was once ever-present in his life as his father lay dying in another room: a memory he's now pushed to the back of his mind, like me getting scared of carry-outs again once I was no longer doing them. I tell him that visiting or not visiting the grave doesn't matter and we agree that his father wouldn't mind anyway. We agree that – as blokes – we often try to look as if we don't care when we do. So not visiting the grave doesn't mean that he doesn't care. We agree that his father will always be in his heart, regardless of whether or not Joey visits the grave.

He organises an abortive attempt to visit the grave with his friends accompanying him (they don't turn up!) before, finally, he manages to visit for the first time on the anniversary of his father's death. He reports that everything was fine. Other people were there and they were joking, which he hadn't expected. He says he might go to the grave on his own next time.

We defend ourselves in various ways against the anxieties provoked in us by physical death. Like Joey, we might avoid cemeteries. Like his friends, we might make jokes. Like hospital porters, we might pretend not to care…

Yalom (1980) describes how, in coping with these anxieties, most people:

> develop adaptive coping modes – modes that consist of denial-based strategies such as suppression, repression, replacement, displacement, belief in personal omnipotence, acceptance of socially sanctioned religious beliefs that 'detoxify' death, or personal efforts to overcome death through a wide variety of strategies that aim at achieving symbolic immortality. (pp.110–11)

Young people might be busily trying to convince themselves that they'll never die, but they remain anxious – just in case!

At the age of three, the psychologist Alfred Adler woke up one morning to find that his younger brother had died in the adjoining bed (Orgler 1975). Then, two years later, Adler himself developed pneumonia and was given no chance of surviving. He recovered but, understandably, found himself afraid of death as he walked to school every day through a cemetery near the family home. 'One day I made up my mind to put an end to this fear of death,' he wrote. 'I decided on a method to harden myself. I lingered behind the other [children], placed my school bag on the ground near the cemetery wall and ran across it a dozen times until I felt I had mastered the fear. After that I believe that I passed along this path without any fear' (p.23). Later in life, Adler found out from former school friends that no cemetery had ever existed on their way to school. Evidently he'd constructed this 'memory' in order to overcome his fear of death.

Young people find plenty of ways like these of defending themselves against thinking about physical death, but it's a thought that keeps coming back, however obliquely. They have endless discussions about abortion, for example:

'You're killing a child!'

'No, you're not! It's so small it hardly exists!'

'Makes no difference! It's still a child. And you're killing it!'

These conversations are always driven by the unacknowledged thought, 'What if it was me? What if I'd been aborted?' Young people are equally exercised about peers who cut themselves or take overdoses, feeling sorry for them but also scornful, scared but also intrigued:

'I don't know how anyone could do that!'

'But you would, wouldn't you, if you were that desperate…'

'No! I can't imagine ever being so desperate that I'd try to kill myself!'

'You don't know. You might be!'

'Maybe, but I'd never be able to go through with it.'

'Hannah Williams tried to kill herself!'

'What, you mean ten paracetamol? That's not exactly trying to kill yourself!'

'She still had to go to hospital and have her stomach pumped.'

'I know! I'd hate that. There'd be all these people wanting to know why you did it and did you really mean to kill yourself…'

'If I was going to kill myself, I'd do it! I wouldn't stop after ten paracetamol!'

'That's because you're so hard!'

'No, I'm not saying that. I'm just saying that, if you're going to do it, you do it…'

And so the conversation goes on, with young people nagging away at something they can't quite put into words: their fear of death and fascination with death. They may have no experience of physical death in their lives, but mention physical *injury* to any group of young people and they're off, the stories tumbling out – arms and legs broken, shoulders dislocated, nights in hospital, bandages, stitches, slings, plaster casts, crutches, enormous cuts, bruises everywhere – stories told with relish…

'Did it hurt?'

'Not really!'

Stories told with enough energy to suggest that there might be something more anxious behind the excited faces, the nervous laughter. Ask young people about the prospect of physical death and most will defend themselves immediately: 'I'm not scared of dying! Doesn't bother me!' Apparently, they never lack for courage when it comes to death…

3

COURAGE AND DEATH

Young people talk about courage a lot, admiring people who are brave and scorning people who are cowardly. They're forever daring each other to do brave things ('Bet you'd never have the guts!') while privately berating themselves, feeling that they *should* have the guts, they *should* be more courageous.

Becker (1973) argues that physical heroism has traditionally been a way of dealing with the threat of death. Charging off into battle, the brave hero proves that he's not scared and that death is of little consequence. His heroism will conquer or at least nullify the threat of death. But nowadays, Becker continues, heroism is much harder to define. For most young people, there are no longer wars to fight or initiation ceremonies to survive. Their need to conquer the fear of death hasn't changed, but heroism is no longer such a straightforward way of trying to do it. In the absence of armies, young people can join street gangs and go to war with each other. They can dare each other to do brave things, but, for most, getting drunk will be the closest they come to acts of physical heroism. With a drink inside, all sorts of things are possible. Alcoholic grandiosity obliterates any potential cowardice.

'I don't give a shit!' says Declan. 'They can say what they want! I'm not doing it!'

'Because if you did, then they'd have won?'

'Yeah! I'm not going to be treated like that!'

'More than your life's worth…'

'Yeah! I'm not changing how I am for anyone!'

Boys tell brave stories, exaggerating where necessary to achieve the desired effect. In their stories they're warriors, no longer needing their mothers – hell, no! Rather, they're brave warriors who've survived against all the odds, lying on the pavement now, too drunk to stand and tended by their upset girlfriends.

Tom looks at me portentously. 'I told my little brother not to be like me.'

'Why?'

'Because of all the stupid things I've done. I've ruined my life, haven't I!'

He hasn't ruined his life but he'd like me to know that he bears a few scars. Years ago, he might have had a James Dean poster on his wall – melancholy, misunderstood, tragic Tom, always sticking up for the underdog and terribly, terribly attractive. The girls love Tom. The more heroically self-destructive he is – getting excluded from school, getting stoned, getting arrested, getting kicked out of home – the more he excites their sympathy as he falls battered and bleeding into their arms. 'Oh Tom!'

Big J is different. He's a football warrior, telling me heroic stories in which the opposition players are all huge, racist thugs, but Big J fights back and teaches them a lesson. Until, that is, he's sent off for calling the referee a wanker.

Keef's heroism involves taking the blame for other people 'because they're my mates!' Like some wrongly accused prisoner, Keef is always keen to sacrifice himself, protecting his mates to the last.

Implicit in the heroics of Declan, Tom, Big J, Keef and hundreds of others is the need to be remembered. Like rock stars dying young, the heroism of these boys is also about meeting an untimely end (expelled from school, sent off the pitch, punished despite being innocent…) and going out in a blaze of glory. With people watching. And remembering.

In addition to the physical heroes, there are the academic ones. Every year thousands of apprentice heroes and heroines go off to university, all claiming to be really looking forward to it. Months later, they return as fully fledged, conquering heroes having (apparently) made loads of new friends, got drunk loads of times and done loads of other crazy things so heroic that they can't possibly be described to uninitiated cowards languishing at home. ('Just look at the pictures on Facebook!') No one tells the other story – the one about feeling homesick, left out, bewildered, embarrassed, stupid – because no self-respecting hero or heroine would admit to such feelings.

Heroism is one way of dealing with transition and loss, and young people's lives are certainly filled with all sorts of losses (Luxmoore 2006, 2010). Declan's father is in prison; Tom's parents have been on the verge of splitting up for years; Big J has moved schools six times; Keef has never met his father. The academic heroes are losing the safety of a school where they were known and admired, but sooner or later *all* young people – whatever their circumstances – are obliged to face up to various kinds of loss. One response is to crumble and give up but – for most young people – that's cowardice. The alternative, therefore, is to fight heroically against the invisible enemy responsible for all these losses (fate? death?) and fight by becoming larger and louder than anyone else, becoming teenage warriors like Declan, faced with impossible odds and screaming at the world, 'I don't give a shit!'

Neil comes to see me because of a history of angry outbursts which get him into trouble. He comes willingly enough but today looks furious, even as he insists that everything is 'all right'.

I ask how things are between him and his father.

'All right.'

I ask how school has been since we last met.

'All right.'

For a long time he was badly bullied by his older brothers. I ask how those relationships have been.

His eyes scan the wall opposite. He tries really hard, casting around for something different to say.

'All right.'

I'm stumped, wondering how to help him through this impasse without drawing attention to his inarticulacy or making him feel that he's getting counselling wrong, the way he gets so many other things in his life wrong. At a loss, I ask about his mother's fish, remembering that her boyfriend keeps them and that she's recently started keeping fish herself.

He relaxes at last. She's just bought a Japanese fighting fish.

I confess my ignorance.

He explains that Japanese fighting fish will fight each other 'to the death' and that's why his mother can only have one of these fish in the tank at a time.

I don't know whether to speculate with him about the symbolic meaning of this. Might the idea of fish fighting each other 'to the death' represent something of his relationship with his brothers? Or represent something about wanting to kill his father who, after several affairs, finally went off with one of the women? Or might this simply mean that Neil experiences counselling as a fight in which he's always on his own?

I think it's more likely that these fish represent a kind of heroism – the heroism of the lone warrior, needing and relying on no one, afraid of no one, programmed from birth to be completely self-reliant. This is how Neil currently sees the world: it would be impossible for more than one fish (Neil and his brothers) to co-exist in the maternal tank without fighting, and that fight would have to be to the death. Forget any stupid notions of brotherly love!

Helping him to think about these things (love, death, hatred, survival) instead of being merely *powered by* them will be our therapeutic task. Neil will be less likely to enact his feelings and get himself into trouble if he can learn to name them and think about them with another person. But in the meantime, as our conversation flags again, I suggest that we play Pigs.

He looks curious.

I get the game out of my bag and explain the rules. Like dice, you throw the two little plastic pigs and how they land determines your score. You can safeguard your score by banking it or you can keep throwing to get a bigger and bigger score but, in so doing, you risk losing your current score if the pigs land in a particular way. First player to a hundred wins.

He smiles, intrigued.

We play the game and he lights up, realising that it doesn't require any brainpower. He loves it. We finish two games before our session ends and, the next time we meet, he immediately asks to play again.

We keep talking and we keep playing Pigs. I come to realise that playing Pigs is just as important as talking because, when we play, we play together: Neil no longer feels so alone and *that's* why he smiles, *that's* why he relaxes, *that's* why he's no longer monosyllabic in our sessions. Yalom (1980) writes that it's 'a profound human paradox: we yearn for autonomy but recoil from autonomy's invisible consequence – isolation' (p.251). I think Neil was protecting himself from feeling the loss of family relationships by becoming a Japanese fighting fish, but the price of being a Japanese fighting fish was to feel terribly, terribly lonely.

With losses like Neil's stored inside them, there are lots of young people who sit in my counselling room telling exaggeratedly heroic tales. I don't ask why they need to exaggerate because I know. And I don't ask what they're afraid of because, for most, admitting to fear of any kind is admitting to cowardice. They're forever afraid: afraid of not fighting, of not succeeding, of not surviving. There's a train of thought that links these fears to feeling worthless to feeling invisible to not existing, the greatest fear of all (see Chapter 5).

On the table in my room is a Russian doll with six smaller dolls inside it. Young people are forever dismantling and reassembling this doll and sometimes, instead of asking explicitly about their fear, I use an exercise learned from the psychotherapist Marcia Karp.

I give the doll to the young person and ask, 'What do you have too much of in your life?'

'Hassle from my parents!' they might say.

I invite them to remove the first layer of the doll and, as they do so, I say, 'If I didn't have so much hassle from my parents, then…?'

'Then I'd be happier.'

I invite them to remove the second layer of the doll. 'If I was happier, then…?'

'Then I'd get on better with my schoolwork.'

They remove the third layer.

'If I got on better with my schoolwork, then…?'

'Then I'd get on better with my parents.'

The fourth layer of doll is removed. It's getting smaller.

'If I got on better with my parents, then…?'

'Then they'd trust me more.'

The fifth layer is removed.

'If they trusted me more…?'

'Then I'd trust them.'

Sixth layer.

'If I trusted them…?'

'Then I'd love them.'

We've reached the tiny baby doll inside. There are no more layers. The young person is thoughtful and moved.

We pause.

'What happens now?'

'We build it back up again. What do you need *more* of in your life?'

'Appreciation!'

'Put the next layer back onto the doll. If I was more appreciated, then…?'

'Then I'd be happier!'

'And the next layer. If I was happier, then…?'

'Then I'd have more friends and see more people. Go to more parties.'

'Next layer. If I had more friends and saw more people, then…?'

'Then more people would know what I'm really like.'

'Next layer. If more people knew what I'm really like, then…?'

'Then I'd enjoy my life.'

'Next layer. If I enjoyed my life…?'

'Then I'd get on better with my parents.'

With the last layer added, the Russian doll is complete again, the young person symbolically rebuilt. It's a powerful exercise and I let the young person settle for a few minutes afterwards, thinking about it. I don't make didactic, and-so-you-see teaching points. Instead, the young person makes his or her own connections… 'It's all to do with my parents!' The experience of *physically* removing the layers of the doll adds an emotional dimension, stripping the young person back to something much more primitive and childlike before then reassembling the doll and, in so doing, giving the young person back his or her necessary defences. We don't talk about courage or cowardice, but the young person has dared to show me something of what lies beneath all those brave, I-don't-give-a-shit protestations.

What lies beneath is the need to survive and grow and, as part of that growing process, to usurp our parents. Out of the blue, Stefan's father left home a year ago to live with a neighbour he'd been seeing for years, unbeknown to anyone in the family. Angry and afraid, thirteen-year-old Stefan has refused to speak to his father ever since and now, a year or so later, regales me with apparently unconnected stories of physical defiance and bravery – go-carts, shotguns, motorbikes, dangling from trees, falling down quarries. I put a lot of misplaced effort into trying to draw him back to the subject of his father before realising that these physically heroic stories – told to me with a smile of satisfaction – are actually the roundabout ways in which Stefan is responding to his father. In effect, they're ways of preparing for manhood: ways of getting stronger, readying himself for the day when he'll confront his father as a physical equal. And when that day comes, they probably *won't* fight – I'm sure that Stefan isn't literally planning to kill his father to avenge his mother's distress – but knowing that he *could* fight and match his father if he wanted will make Stefan feel a whole lot better.

We use courage as a way of dealing with threats to our existence. No one dies of cancer nowadays except 'bravely' and 'fighting to the end' (Diamond 1998). Emboldened by this rhetoric, we try not to feel impotent in the face of death. Stefan experiences an event (his father leaving) that challenges his potency, his ability to control his life. To a young person, this can feel like a matter of life or death and therefore like an event to which he or she must respond courageously. Yet the need to be courageous and the possibility of being cowardly go hand in hand, leaving young people anxious. Boys might be particularly interested in developing their physical prowess – play-fighting, arm wrestling and surviving other physical tests – but boys and girls also face emotional and moral challenges, all of which can feel like a choice between courage and cowardice. The job of a professional might be to encourage in young people a more relaxed bearing of both possibilities: I can be brave sometimes and afraid at other times. That's normal!

Without that encouragement, there are boys with a haphazard sense of their own power: omnipotent one minute and utterly helpless the next. At the age of thirteen, Stefan was suddenly challenged by his father – physically and (by implication) sexually – to a contest he could never win, a contest in which he was completely powerless to stop his father leaving his mother and sleeping with another woman. In psychoanalytical terms, his potency was shamed. He couldn't beat up his father or steal his father's girlfriend, so he had to find some thirteen-year-old way of asserting his power. Psychoanalytically, he killed his father ('You're nothing to me!') by refusing to see him. That was the bravest, most hostile thing he could do. Yet despite this, the courage-versus-cowardice anxiety hasn't gone away for Stefan, just as it doesn't go away for other boys who spend time searching for authority figures against whom they can test their potency in safe and gradual ways. Stefan might have done more extreme things. He might have fought with his school or with the police or with his enemies; he might have cut or tried to kill himself; he might have curled up in a corner, stoned and lifeless. However extreme the behaviour, his anxiety would have remained because young people can never decide whether fighting and self-harming are courageous or cowardly acts. Fighting is admired by some yet scorned by others; self-harming is seen either as 'having the guts' or as 'being pathetic'.

Courageously killing off a parent ('He's nothing to me! I'm never speaking to him again! I'm certainly never *seeing* him again!') is always a way of protecting ourselves from what we anticipate will be extinction at the hands of that parent. It's a primitive attempt to survive, triumphing over death. And, for a short while, the illusion of triumph holds before we succumb to the knowledge that – alive or dead – we can never entirely banish these authority figures from our heads. So better to find some way of beginning to talk about them, a counsellor might suggest. Better to try and understand our fears.

4

DEATH AS AN AUTHORITY FIGURE

We've been talking about Mehdi's decision to get a job rather than continue at school. 'The leavers' party will be the last thing before I leave this place,' he says. 'After that, no one'll remember me. They'll say they will but they won't.'

Instead of assuring him that, on the contrary, he'll never be forgotten, I agree with him. 'You're right. They'll remember you for a while, Mehdi. Some people will remember you for a long time but eventually they'll forget you just like they'll forget me and everyone else.' I tell him about Thomas Hardy's poem 'His Immortality', with its blunt account of the way in which a dead person is remembered, remembered and then finally forgotten as the last remembering person dies.

'It's weird,' he says, 'but that's actually true!'

We talk about his grandfathers, both of whom died before he was born; about them living on in his parents' memories and how Mehdi himself might be a grandfather one day, living on in someone's memory.

'That's such a head fuck!'

We laugh, but it's important to be talking about these things. I think they've been bubbling away inside Mehdi for ages, unconsciously informing his rows with teachers, his sense of life's unfairness and his inability to decide between a life of purposeful engagement or hedonistic abandon. I tell him about Yalom's (2008) idea that we create ripples: the people we were and the things we did in our lives become ripples spreading outwards, still dispersing long after we're dead and no longer able to see what became of our efforts – our small, rippling effects on the world.

He has one grandfather who worked hard all his life before dying of a heart attack and another who drank himself to death: two men creating very different kinds of ripples. 'It depends on the ripples,' he says. 'Some ripples might be remembered more than others!'

Like anyone, his fear of not being remembered is primitive. It would feel like not existing, like being dead. Like anyone, he needs to be seen and recognised to feel that he exists and is worth something (Luxmoore 2008). Mehdi is academically talented but, in spite of that, plans to leave school and get a job. That way, he'll continue to be recognised locally in the streets and bars, whereas going away to university sounds to him like being unrecognised, like being indistinguishable from other people. 'I wouldn't know what to say to a bunch of students,' he says. 'I wouldn't know where I was supposed to go. They'd probably think I was the waiter or something and tell me to go and get them a drink!'

I remind him of three dreams he's told me about during the weeks that we've been meeting. In one, he was a rock star playing to a large audience. In another, he was a caterpillar being stamped on by a large boot and, in the third dream, he was arguing with his boss in an office. I ask whether the first and second dreams might be about power and powerlessness. They happen to be images of a grandiose rock star and a helpless caterpillar but their significance might be that they represent extremes of visibility and invisibility, of power and powerlessness. I suggest that the third dream (the row with the boss) might represent an argument with death or with God or with whoever decides our fates because, despite our best attempts to be rock stars, we usually end up as squashed caterpillars, invisible and unrecognised by the big boss. We're forever fighting against a fate inflicted on us by the boss who can never be outmanoeuvred.

There's a boss-like authority about death. Whenever young people are fighting with the everyday authority figures in their lives, I think there's a sense in which they're always fighting obliquely with death. 'Why does it have to be this way? Why can't you make an exception for me? Why don't I have a say? Who gives you the right to make these decisions about my life, and, if it's always going to be like this, then what's the point?'

Mehdi fights for recognition, afraid of being crushed, killed off. Faith, a year younger than Mehdi, fights with the school system to prove that she isn't afraid of it and doesn't care. Her fighting certainly gets her recognised but, at the same time, does her no favours: she's rude to teachers, gets into trouble with the police and rows constantly with her mother at home. 'It's so unfair!' she complains.

I agree with her that things in her life *have* been unfair. They may not have been anyone's fault but they've been unfair nonetheless. She didn't deserve her parents' fighting. Or her stepbrother's bullying. Or her kidney problems which are refusing to go away. I assure her that although she may have been powerless at earlier times in her life, she does now have some power: the power to get herself excluded from school. Her teachers can try their best to support her; they can think up all kinds of helpful strategies to stop her getting into trouble, but, ultimately, she can get herself excluded if she chooses.

For Faith, this experience of having power is exciting but scary. When they fight at home, her mother always gives in and Faith always wins. 'My mum spoils me,' she says, embarrassed, well aware that she shouldn't be winning all the time. So, having beaten her mother, she transfers her fight to a more robust enemy called 'school', where she can properly test her strength. At school, teachers resist her power, fighting her at every turn. Her sense of this 'school' she's forever fighting is about much more than just a set of buildings and teachers: this 'school' in her head is a mother, a father, a whole world of fairness and unfairness (Luxmoore 2008). She rages, daring it to do its worst, wondering if it'll carry out its threats, wondering if it really cares. She tries to outsmart it. She pleads for special privileges and, when 'school' won't oblige, she rails against its non-negotiable, 'unfair' authority. In her fights with 'school', she can certainly get herself excluded but, as with the authority of death, she can never win.

She could give up. Excluded from school, she could surrender herself to a life of abject drug taking and daytime television, refusing to engage with life and effectively committing a kind of suicide, letting death do whatever it wants: 'I don't give a shit! See if I care!' The alternative to abject surrender or endless fighting would be to find some way of living with the seeming unfairness of authority while still finding satisfaction in her life, of living in an imperfect world but creating all kinds of interesting ripples.

'I don't care!' she keeps saying.

I make a comment about school refusing to go away.

'Yeah, I know, but I don't care!'

Fighting her assertion ('I'm sure you do care really, Faith!') would be pointless. Of course she cares, but this is really about her determination not to feel powerless. I remind her of the unfair things in her life – her parents, her stepbrother, her kidneys. 'I wonder why unfair things happen?'

'Because life sucks?' she says. 'I don't know. How should I know?'

We both smile.

'Life does suck,' I say, 'especially when unfair things happen which aren't our fault, which we never asked to happen and which we can't control!'

She agrees.

'And there are *lots* of things we can't control…'

'I suppose.'

'Things that are annoying and unfair and things that we haven't got any power to do anything about.'

She looks unconvinced.

I remind her of the prayer that goes, 'Lord, grant me the serenity to accept the things I can't change, courage to change the things I can and wisdom to know the difference.'

She doesn't understand.

'It's like fighting the battles we have to fight and *not* fighting the ones we don't have to fight and can never win.'

'Yeah,' she says, 'but school really pisses me off!'

'I know it does,' I say, 'but the trouble is that school will always win. It has to win to survive.'

'So do I!'

We both laugh and move on to talking about other things. But, like bursting into tears or bursting into anger, our laughter is cathartic: it's a release, a kind of acceptance. Faith knows that I approve in principle of her feistiness. Laughing together, we acknowledge the impossibility of the

– 49 –

situation: Faith's stubbornness versus the stubbornness of 'school'. She has her power but so does 'school': she can never be the outright winner. Despite her attempts to destroy it, 'school' will be there long after she's gone.

Any young person's relationship with 'school' is always part of a broader relationship with authority and – deep down – with the authority of death. All Faith's battles about rules, rules, rules and the unfairness of rules are ultimately about death because death is the ultimate authority figure, the rule that can never be broken. Paradoxically, we're imprisoned but also liberated by death. 'Death destroys a man: the idea of Death saves him,' writes E. M. Forster (1910, 1992, p.250). For young people, growing older involves trying to understand this paradox. How exactly can rules of any kind liberate us? Surely freedom means having no rules at all? The rules young people fight about – bedtimes, computer use and seeing friends, for example – are only the tip of an iceberg. There are official, explicit rules such as 'Say please and thank you!' and 'I want you in by nine o'clock!' but there are dozens of other unofficial, unspoken, *implicit* rules such as 'Never get angry with Dad!' and 'Don't ask questions about the past!' These implicit rules underpin everything and they're much harder to understand because no one ever writes them down or explains how they came about. Death is an implicit rule:

'Why do we have to die?'

'Because everyone dies!'

'I know, but why?'

As young people get older and more powerful, they're passionately engaged in a long-term research project far more important than any coursework or exams: they're researching rules. How did the rules come about? Why do they exist? Who invented them? How flexible are they?

Who enforces them? What are the consequences of breaking them?

Professionals running groups for young people are usually keen to make the rules of the group clear from the start so that the young people in the group feel safe and behave well. And, as part of the group's learning, they want the young people themselves to be involved in making the rules. So, after everyone has introduced themselves, the first session typically starts with a rule-making exercise. 'What about confidentiality? What about nicknames? Do we need a rule about not interrupting or a rule about everyone having an equal say? What do you think...?'

The exercise falls on anxious ears. The rules eventually agreed and written down with the encouragement of the professional mean little because – as yet – the group has no idea what rules it might need for itself. It's too early in its lifetime to know what to expect or what dangers might be thrown up by this experience. Like a new-born baby, the fledgling group needs its mother to make all the decisions. It's still merged with her and reliant on her. Only once it gains in confidence and begins to separate from her, learning to think for itself, can it cope with the responsibility of starting to regulate itself, and *that's* the time to start negotiating rules.

But by then various rules will have been established in any case – *implicit* rules about things like teasing, favouritism, talking and not talking about personal things, being clever, being left out, disagreeing with each other... These implicit rules were never discussed or written down by the group and yet they're more important than the explicit rules the group did discuss such as being on time, not swearing and always trying to respect each other.

Rules regulate for us a world of opportunity and frustration, of things we can do and things we can't do. We might want to live forever, but the biggest rule of all says that we have to die. And this is the implicit rule that no one will talk about, the rule established and enforced…by whom? Who invented it? Who can we argue with about changing such an unfair rule? Young people want to know why the rules exist and, if there isn't a good-enough reason, then why not? 'Why do we have to die? Why?'

Jessi says she did it because she'd had enough. Her friends had turned against her because she'd given a blow job to the boy who was supposed to be going out with Natalie.

'Which wasn't true!' she says. '*And* there was a rumour going round that I was pregnant, which wasn't true, and now they're saying I've got chlamydia!'

A few days ago, she'd had enough of all this. She deliberately cut into her arm.

When I ask to see the cut, she rolls up her sleeve nervously and shows me a scratch. I try to look impressed, glad that I won't have to tell anybody about such a small scratch but also wanting Jessi to know that she's being taken seriously because, when it feels as if all your friends have turned against you, that really does feel horrible. Living with the ebb and flow of friendships is a preoccupation for all young people – learning the implicit rules, learning what you can and can't control, learning about the effects of your words and actions, learning to deal with the uncertainty of life and the certainty of death.

'All I said was that I *quite* fancied him! I didn't say I wanted to go out with him. Christ, I do *know* that he's going out with Natalie! I'm not stupid!'

'But they thought you meant it about fancying him?'

'Yeah, they always take things the wrong way!'

'Maybe you were curious, Jessi?'

'What do you mean?'

'Maybe you were curious to see what would happen if people knew that you quite fancied him…'

'Why would I want to do that?'

'Because we're always curious about things. Because that's normal. We're always wondering what it would be like if things were different. We're always seeing how far we can go. I think it's good to be curious. The difficult thing is that, being curious, we get hurt sometimes.'

'You can say that again!' she says. 'I wish I hadn't said anything. I wish I'd kept my stupid mouth shut!'

She's been testing the implicit rule decreeing that you don't flirt with your best friend's boyfriend and you certainly don't give him blow jobs. I wonder how much the self-harming of young people like Jessi is always an attempt to feel more alive, an implicit exploration of death and dying, a testing of personal resolve in the face of physical instinct: Jessi daring to harm herself when her instinct is to protect herself. 'Could I do it? Could I do it *a bit*? How satisfying would it be? How much would it hurt? How would other people react?' The anger that most self-harming young people describe in counselling is usually anger towards some kind of authority – most obviously towards the authority of their parents (the daily rule makers), sometimes towards the social authority of their friends, but I suspect that their anger is ultimately towards the implacable, final authority of death. 'Given that my life won't go on forever, how much authority do I have? How much authority do other people have? I can cut myself… Could I *kill* myself?'

Whether they like it or not, therapists and other professionals working with young people are also authority figures. Langs (1997) argues that anxieties about death are expressed in therapy through 'frame modifications [which] are the primary enacted means through which both patients and therapists attempt to adapt to unresolved death anxieties' (p.56). By 'frame modifications' he means all the ways in which we depart from our norms, our routines, our original rules and agreed ways of behaving together. The implication is that because death is such an absolutely certain, non-negotiable rule, all other rules become unconscious reminders of that big one. In bending these lesser rules, we unconsciously attempt to bend the biggest rule of all, and we do so because we're anxious about dying.

Langs is writing about therapeutic relationships, but his thinking might usefully be applied to other kinds of relationships where we also find ourselves trying to change the rules. I wonder, for example, about relationships in schools where students are *constantly* trying to get teachers to bend the rules and where teachers are *constantly* developing new rules, procedures, protocols and expectations in response. To what extent is school life, with its constant emphasis on 'the future' and on young people's 'unlimited potential', actually defending itself against a pervading anxiety about death and the eventual loss of all those futures? We invest our hopes in young people not only because we love them but also because they'll continue after we're gone. So what does it *really* mean for parents and professionals when a young person fails to fulfil his or her potential (Luxmoore 2008)? It can feel as if the parents and professionals themselves have failed and as if some part of them is in danger of being lost forever. 'You'll never get this chance again!' we say bitterly to young people. Perhaps we create rules partly to minimise the risk of a young person dying physically and partly to minimise the risk of a young person's potential ever dying. In this way, we guard against the dying of our own potential. And yet we're excited whenever an inventor or artist breaks the rules, discovering new ways of understanding or looking at the world. We may curb young people's excesses in order to keep them safe, but we also quite like them to rebel, break world records and change the world. Perhaps we look to them to challenge death on our behalf?

Our children may be our legacies, but young people are keen to leave their own legacies wherever they go – scratching their names onto a park bench or tree as if to ensure that some part of them will remain, even after it's dark and they've gone indoors to watch a film. With no legacy to fall back on, Mehdi worries that he'd be lost at university. Faith desperately tries to leave her mark on 'school'. Jessi's curious to see what the rules will do to her if she breaks them. All three are simultaneously fighting and in flight from the authority of death, all anxious to survive. Schopenhauer (1970) writes, 'We all feel that we are something other than a being which someone once created out of nothing: from this arises the confidence that, while death may be able to end our life, it cannot end our existence' (p.68).

We might want to believe that we'll survive death but we fear otherwise...

5

THE FEAR OF NOT EXISTING

Once upon a time we didn't exist and there are family photographs to prove it. We're missing from all those carefully arranged groupings, from all those wacky moments, and yet the world seems to be managing perfectly well without us. Evidently, we came from nowhere and will go back to nowhere. 'After your death you will be what you were before your birth,' writes Schopenhauer (1970, p.67).

It's the thought of ceasing to exist when we die – the threat of extinction – that bothers young people even more than the prospect of physically dying. In his furious poem 'Aubade', Philip Larkin (2003) describes the uselessness of religion, sensuality, courage, rationality and attachment as ways of dealing with the 'sure extinction' awaiting us. For Larkin, there are no consolations, no ways of avoiding the mundane fate awaiting us all.

The prospect of their 'sure extinction' propels young people into all sorts of behaviours that, at first glance, seem unrelated to death. There are visible behaviours such as fighting with knives, drinking far too much, cutting or poisoning themselves, smoking despite the dangers – behaviours all of which flirt with the possibility of death. And there are invisible behaviours such as hiding away in front of the television all day, slumped and miserable, avoiding physical risk of any sort – behaviours that seem designed to avoid death by effectively avoiding life. 'Neurosis is the way of avoiding non-being by avoiding being,' writes Tillich (1952, p.66): if we never invest our hopes in anything, if we never really commit ourselves to anything, then we'll never be disappointed and never feel the pain of loss. Visibly or invisibly, through behaviours larger than life or smaller than life, smashing up against the wall of death or trying to sneak under it, young people fight death overtly or are in flight from it.

Their third response is to freeze. Lifton (1974) describes people protecting themselves from anxieties about death through 'psychic numbing'. These people cut themselves off from feeling and thinking anything. They're stuck. They know perfectly well that they can't go back to childhood but they're afraid to move forwards for fear of the unknown or, perhaps, for fear of the *very* known. Gersie (1991) tells an old Tewa Indian story where, once upon a time, people lived in deep darkness under the earth. This was all they knew and all they expected to know until a few of them became dissatisfied and began to wonder whether this was all there was.

They asked the Mole who seemed able to come and go as he pleased. He replied that, yes, his burrowing suggested that there was indeed another, lighter world, but, because he was blind, he couldn't see it.

The people were curious. They decided to leave their homes and follow the burrowing Mole, setting off behind him, passing the earth back to those behind who, in turn, passed it back.

Eventually they emerged into a terrible, blinding light. They covered their eyes, instinctively wanting to run back to their homes. But their way had long since been blocked by the earth they'd been heaping behind them, filling the tunnel. They realised that they'd never be able to find their way back to their homes but, at the same time, they knew that they couldn't remain where they were, blinded by the terrifying light. Panicking, they argued with each other until the little old Spider Woman spoke. She suggested that they face the light and take their hands away from their eyes. But a little at a time. Slowly. And patiently.

It hurt to do this, but they did as she suggested, moving their hands away from their eyes a little at a time, a little more each time, until at last their eyes became used to the light and they could see.

Counselling might be one way in which young people dare – a little at a time, slowly, patiently – to look ahead at what awaits them. Having felt stuck and having waited, waited, waited, most young people eventually kick-start their own lives. But others need help to unfreeze: not help of the enraged kind ('You're wasting your life! When are you actually going to *do* something?') but of a gentler, more collaborative kind ('Life's scary, isn't it! It's tempting to hide under the duvet!'). Perhaps counsellors are really little old Spider Women, making suggestions and helping young people adapt to the new worlds awaiting them.

However they adapt – through fight, flight, freeze or through some less obvious defensive manoeuvre – young people's fear of extinction remains primitive. A baby must be recognised by its mother from the moment of its birth in order to survive and eventually develop a sense of self (Winnicott 1971). It feels terrible to go unrecognised, unheard, unnoticed, and so a baby will do anything – clinging desperately, screaming all night long – in order to be recognised. 'If I'm recognised, then I exist and I'm safe. If I'm recognised, then my needs can be met and I can relax. But if I'm *un*recognised, then no one will care for me, no one will look after me and – sooner or later – I'll die.' Our survival depends on being recognised by our external environment. Following Herder and Hegel, Schopenhauer (1969) argues that there's no such thing as an individual, as 'I', except in relation to something else. He pre-dates Winnicott's (1964) joke that 'there's no such thing as a baby' (p.88): the idea that a baby can only exist in relation to its mother, the way a mother can only be a mother if she has a child. By extension, we can only begin to exist as individuals if other people exist, mirroring us back to ourselves, confirming and recognising our existence.

So much of young people's behaviour stems from this earliest anxiety about existing and not existing. Through their words and behaviour, they're always trying to be heard, noticed, understood, recognised. Often, they'll insist that they don't consciously think about death, and yet their most vehement behaviour will always express an underlying need for recognition: see me! hear me! feel me! touch me! and, most importantly, *understand me!* so that I can relax, knowing that I'm connected with other people, no longer alone, no longer unrecognised, no longer in danger of extinction.

Duncan-John says, 'To be honest, I don't think about death that much. But when I do die, I'd like to have made an impact.' In his family culture, it's important to stand out, to be visibly successful, and so making an impact will prove that he existed as far as his family was concerned.

Yvonne says, 'I don't think about death! No way! But I do think about *how* I'm going to die. I want to die like in *Titanic*, when I'm old…' I think she means that she'd like to be an old woman with a loving family around her bedside, proving that she matters, because Yvonne's life so far has been a story of apparently mattering to no one.

Like Duncan-John and Yvonne, we expect our deaths to confirm or disconfirm what we've always believed or wanted to believe about our lives – that we were a burden to other people and no one cared, or that we made an impact, existed and mattered.

Zara believes that no one cares about her. 'If I died, my family wouldn't even bother to turn up at the funeral!' she says. 'They'd be down the pub celebrating!'

Rather than challenge her long-held belief that 'no one cares about me', I ask what she'd want to say if she could speak at her own funeral.

'I'd tell them that I hate them all,' she says, looking at me, wide-eyed, 'and I'm *glad* I'm dead because now I won't have to see them any more!'

'Would they be upset?'

'No! They'd be glad!'

'Glad to be rid of you? Glad to forget you?'

'Too right!' Then, as an afterthought, she adds, 'Except my cousins. They're only small. They'd be sad.'

I ask what her cousins would miss about her.

'They'd miss me playing with them because whenever they come over I'm the only one who ever plays with them!'

'Because you're fun? Because you know what it's like when people *don't* play?'

She thinks about this. 'Probably…'

We've made a start. All we're doing is beginning to recognise parts of Zara that currently feel unrecognised – parts like her ability to have fun and empathise with small children. Over time, there'll be plenty of other parts of Zara to recognise as well – her anger, sadness, emptiness, love of dancing… If she can begin to feel more recognised, she'll be less likely to scream for recognition in a hundred different ways.

Because young people have spent their lives building up a fledgling sense of self that relies on other people recognising and thereby bringing into existence the various parts of that self, death threatens everything, taking away the possibility of continuing recognition. With no one to see us, hear us, feel us, touch us, understand us any longer, we simply won't exist. Already we have a sense of what this might be like: Winnicott (1989) argues that we have a perpetual fear of breakdown, of the disintegration and collapse of our carefully arranged defences, and this fear, he argues, is an unconscious *memory*, a 'fear of a breakdown that has already been experienced' (p.89). The experience isn't new, therefore. We've already experienced and survived it as babies who were originally disintegrated, inchoate and empty before we came into existence and began to develop a sense of self under the recognising gaze of a mother. Death isn't unknown, therefore, Winnicott suggests: it's very much known and we fear it because we remember it.

Faced with the continuing prospect of extinction, we set about 'creating' in a thousand different ways. Unconsciously, we bind ourselves together; we prove our existence by putting our energies into creating whatever will withstand attempts to destroy us. Storr (1972) describes creativity as a defence against anxiety – as a way of finding meaning and purpose in life – while Winnicott (1971) describes 'the creativity that…belongs to being alive' (p.67) because, he writes, 'We find that individuals live creatively and feel that life is worth living or else that they cannot live creatively and are doubtful about the value of living' (p.71). I think this is what Duncan-John means by making an impact and what Yvonne means by dying as an old woman surrounded by loving relatives. Both of them hope to have created something: Duncan John hopes to have created an impact; Yvonne hopes to have created loving relationships.

Young people spend most of their time creating, maintaining, negotiating and (preferably once alternatives are available) ending relationships. It's an all-consuming activity. 'My friends are my life,' says Jolene. 'Without them, I've got nothing!' Kohut (1971) describes as 'selfobjects' those relationships from which we get our sense of recognition, our sense of self. We internalise these relationships and they become part of who we are. They might be relationships with people, with experiences or with things: whatever form they take, the loss of them is tantamount to losing parts of ourselves. A best friend might become such an important part of a young person's life, for example, that the ending of that friendship is devastating. 'Without my friends, I might as well be dead!' says Jolene.

Most young people measure their sense of well-being in terms of the quality and quantity of their friendships. Friendships confirm that we exist and matter. Freud (1914) writes that '…in the last resort, we must begin to love in order not to fall ill' (p.78). Loving friendships bind us together and keep us safe; loving friendships keep us healthy and keep us from despair. I think that the creation of friendships is ultimately a response to death, providing us with recognition and with a sense of achievement.

Whatever the creative project, young people become hugely identified with it because it acts as a bulwark against their own extinction. Besides friendships, they latch on to all sorts of other projects, pouring their passionate energies into them. They raise money in response to environmental disasters, especially disasters involving death; they do dangerous, death-defying stunts like bungee jumping and parachuting; they embark on long-distance ordeals of one sort or another. Often these projects raise money for charities associated with life-threatening illnesses; sometimes they're in memory of a person who's died; sometimes they culminate in the setting up of a (death-defying) memorial to that person. And there are the more commonly creative, everyday ways in which young people prove their existence: by getting pregnant (defying death by creating babies), by making music ('It's the most important thing in my life!'), by writing poetry, skateboarding, painting, training for athletics or working towards all sorts of other goals that have come to mean so much. May (1975) describes creativity as a rage against death, as 'a yearning for immortality' (p.31).

Tyrone comes to see me the week after the school play has finished. He looks washed out and says he feels terrible. For months, he's been pouring his energies into this production and last week, he says, was the best of his life. Everybody loved the show; there were all sorts of people coming up to congratulate him afterwards and the backstage atmosphere was fantastic. 'I got to know so many people! It was like a family.'

'And now?'

'I just feel empty. Like I've got nothing to look forward to...' He sighs. 'To be honest, it's been really hard getting out of bed in the mornings. I know I've got to wait for the next production but that's such a long way ahead! I've got nothing now...'

I'm reminded of the way some people talk about coming alive whenever they walk onto a stage. The production has given Tyrone a heightened sense of recognition, and now he's experiencing the gloom that sets in once it's finished, as he knew it would finish, as everybody knew it would finish. That was probably why the atmosphere on the last night was so feverish and the after-show party so wild, like some manic New Year's Eve event (see Chapter 7) or drunken, crazy wake: an after-show party refusing to end, defying extinction, defying death even as the lights were being turned off by the long-suffering caretaker.

Tyrone's reliance on stage lights to take away his emptiness and fear of invisibility is a dangerous strategy because of this come-down afterwards. As he struggles to deal with a renewed feeling of emptiness, he could easily start looking for 'highs' elsewhere. 'Everything seems so boring at the moment,' he says, sprawling in his chair. 'It's all the same, like nothing good ever happens.'

I ask whether his parents came to see the show. I know that Tyrone is close to his mother but rarely sees his father who lives elsewhere with a new partner and two small sons.

'My mum came but my dad couldn't be bothered. He said he was working, which is what he always says.' Tyrone's sense of being discarded is obvious. 'To be honest, I don't care whether he came to see it or not. Makes no difference to me!'

He *does* care but can't admit it at the moment. I think he'd secretly love his father to see the show; he'd love his father to be impressed; he'd love to be recognised by his father as a talented actor, as a popular member of the cast, as funny, daring, clever. And it hurts like hell when his best efforts go unrecognised by the man whose approval he needs.

'My dad can please himself. Doesn't bother me!'

Extreme defences protect us from extreme danger and extreme hurt. Winnicott (1975) argues that a fear of 'annihilation' comes before a fear of death. A baby isn't consciously aware of physical death in the way that it'll grow up to understand physical death. Instead, it's aware only of the possibility of 'annihilation', the experience of being out of synch with its mother, uncontained by her and alienated from her. Because the baby's very existence depends on its mother, to be without her (or to be without *enough* of her) feels like not existing. 'Annihilation' is a strong word but it evokes the absolute terror that a baby might feel, experiencing this.

Good-enough mothering or what Winnicott calls 'environmental' experience allows a baby to internalise a sense that it exists and is recognised without needing to be constantly reassured by the physical presence of another person: in Tyrone's case, by the physical presence of a father or large audience. Good-enough experience, writes Winnicott (1975), allows a baby:

> ...to begin to exist, to have experience, to build a personal ego, to ride instincts, and to meet with all the difficulties inherent in life. All this feels real to the infant who becomes able to have a self that can eventually even afford to sacrifice spontaneity, even to die. (p.304)

Without that good-enough experience, '...this self that can afford to die never develops' (p.304). What he means is that if – out of that good-enough experience – we develop a secure-enough sense of self, physical death ceases to be such a worry because we know that our 'existence' isn't wholly dependent on our physical bodies. We can 'die', therefore, confident that we still exist.

But without that good-enough experience, a brittle, defensive self emerges to protect against the feeling of emptiness, the threat of annihilation. Tyrone's 'doesn't bother me' is a defensive but necessary self, protecting him from hurt. Together, he and I will try to recognise the hurt; we'll recognise what he really feels about his father and we'll recognise that he is, indeed, a talented actor, a popular member of the cast and so on. The more he can internalise a sense of being recognisable, the more he'll be able to live for longer periods of time without needing external recognition.

I ask him what his father would say if he *had* seen the show.

He shrugs. 'Probably nothing!'

'Because he'd be jealous? Because he wouldn't know what to say? I wonder what he'd *think*?'

Tyrone says nothing.

'I wonder if he'd be proud but wouldn't know how to tell you that...?'

'What d'you mean?'

'Well, he might be amazed and happy and proud of you, but because he's a man and because of what's happened between the two of you, he might not be able to say any of that stuff. It might feel to him like being trapped inside. Seeing you on stage, he might wish that he could be as confident as you but he knows he can't be. He might never have felt confident like that in his life.'

'I'm not confident really,' says Tyrone.

'I know. But your dad probably doesn't realise that. He probably just sees this super-confident-looking son who sometimes fights with him and thinks that's all there is to know. He probably thinks that's the whole truth.'

Tyrone thinks about this. I give him plenty of time because if we can see ourselves as others see us and see others the way they see themselves, we can understand and forgive a lot.

Sherry thinks that people like Tyrone who act in school plays are 'pathetic attention seekers'. She'd never bother with anything like that herself. 'It's stupid the way they all go round thinking they're something special!' she says. 'Like they're part of some pathetic club!'

Her cynicism is hard to bear (I keep wanting to tell her how wrong she is!), but I wonder whether it's hard for Sherry to bear her own cynicism. I wonder whether there's a part of her, hidden away, that would love to be part of a school play, would love to be creative in that way and so feel more recognised, less afraid. Heidegger (1962) writes about *unheimlichkeit* – the experience of not being at home in the world, of not belonging: an experience stemming from our awareness of death. Feeling unrecognised in his family, Tyrone enjoys being part of a stage family because, in spending hours and hours rehearsing together, this new family gives him a temporary feeling of being at home in the world. Sherry eschews that experience, mocking it, wary of belonging to anything. She may have a vivid sense of how wonderful experiences like Tyrone's might be but she's stuck with the knowledge that they always come to an end. Meltzer and Harris Williams (1988) argue that our sense of the wonderful possibilities of life is learned from an original experience of our mothers as wholly wonderful, wholly beautiful, and of ourselves as basking in that reflected beauty. However, 'the apprehension of beauty contains in its very nature the apprehension of the possibility of its destruction,' they write (p.6). All young people are haunted by the memory of a better world or promised land somewhere over the rainbow (Luxmoore 2011) and they live with an acute awareness of its loss. They miss it. They mourn it. They get angry thinking about it. The world that once seemed beautiful and bountiful now seems withholding and punitive. Spiky-haired Sherry may be scornful because nothing ever measures up to that beautiful paradise, that maternal idyll she lost and has never recovered.

'I can't see the point,' she says. 'They're only doing it because they know the teachers will love them and because this school thinks it's so great at doing plays. It's pathetic!'

'You've never thought of being in a play?'

'Are you joking? Do me a favour!'

Her vehemence gives her away. 'I suppose you gave up doing that stuff a long time ago?'

'You're right!' she says. 'A very long time ago!'

'What happened?'

'What d'you mean, what happened?'

'What happened to make you stop doing stuff like that?'

'Nothing! I just didn't want to do it!'

'Because of other people? Because of what they'd say?'

'No! I just didn't want to do it! Anyway, why are you asking?'

'Because I'm curious,' I say. 'You're clever and I imagine that you'd be good at acting if you wanted. So I'm interested in what made you stop doing those things...'

She thinks about this, deciding whether or not to abort the conversation. 'If you really want to know, I couldn't be bothered! I used to do drama and stuff like that a long time ago, but then the teacher started picking on me and I stopped going.'

After several years of feuding, her parents split up when Sherry was ten. She's told me very little about this time, but I know that when she started secondary school she was a very different girl from the scornful one now criticising school plays. In those days she kept herself to herself, had few obvious friends and said little in class, like someone shut down or numb, someone disillusioned. I imagine that, once upon a time, Sherry was a little girl loving and trusting her life. Things changed and she found herself hating all the changes, all the broken promises and all the people responsible for them. A wonderful world was lost and replaced by a world of hatred and hostility. So, with sarcasm and cynicism, she now looks to kill off anything hopeful and enthusiastic because it hurts too much to be reminded of the world as it was.

Our sense of a better world never goes away. I ask whether she ever imagines returning to her old interest in drama.

'There'd be no point,' she says. 'I'm not a kid any more! What would be the point of that?'

I say that it's hard to know the point of anything.

She seems reassured by this. 'Still,' she says, 'you might as well make the most of your life while you've got it, eh! Might as well have a laugh!'

'Have a laugh and see what happens...'

'Yeah! No point moping about!'

She and Tyrone seem to have nothing in common but are opposite sides of the same coin: he building things up, creating; she knocking things down, destroying. Freud (1920) proposed the existence of a 'life instinct' forever doing battle with a 'death instinct', the way we spend our lives creating and destroying just as we ourselves were once created and will eventually be destroyed. Tyrone is desperate to be involved in school plays, yet his enthusiasm is powered by his need for recognition as a way of avoiding invisibility. Sherry's cynicism may suggest otherwise, but the relationship she's building with me in counselling is actually what Bollas (1999) calls 'psychic creation': a way of creating a sense of oneself in relationship to another person, like a baby gradually developing a sense of itself out of good-enough mothering experience. If Sherry wasn't interested in making a relationship with me, she wouldn't bother to turn up for appointments. I don't tell her this because I don't want to embarrass her. She (privately) and Tyrone (publicly) are both busy creating because they're both aware of the possibilities of annihilation: Tyrone calls that annihilation 'emptiness'; Sherry calls it 'pointlessness'.

Sherry speaks especially disparagingly about her father, blaming him for everything, and I find myself wondering… If our first loss is of an idealised mother, perhaps death comes to seem like a father, intruding on that original mother–baby reverie, breaking it up and taking away from us the thing we prize most – our mother, our life giver. In most artistic portrayals, death is masculine and, culturally, it's hard for us to associate mothers with death. We don't like to imagine mothers as murderers, for example (Weldon 1988). 'That's unnatural,' we say. 'A mother creates life; she doesn't destroy it.' I wonder about the fact that in primary schools young people are surrounded by mother figures – in the classroom and at the school gates – whereas in secondary schools, with a preponderance of male teachers, young people are increasingly surrounded by father figures. Do young people sense that a maternal, life-giving force is being replaced by a paternal, life-denying one?

Sherry talks a lot about escaping to her grandmother's house and helping out with things. 'The reason I go round there,' she says, 'is because she doesn't hassle me all the time. I can do my homework there and she actually cooks stuff I like! You can tell her things because she doesn't get arsey all the time. She's been through a lot in her life. Nothing fazes her. I don't know what I'd do if I couldn't go round there…'

If young people are full of life instinct and death instinct, always creating and always destroying, grandparents offer them an opportunity to express concern and kindness, to make amends for having behaved in hateful, destructive ways. Winnicott (1971) writes that:

> In the total unconscious fantasy belonging to growth at puberty and in adolescence, there is *the death of someone...* [And] in the psychotherapy of the individual adolescent... there is to be found death and personal triumph as something inherent in the process of maturation and in the acquisition of adult status. (p.145)

What he's suggesting is that, like butterflies breaking out of cocoons, we kill off our parents (psychologically) in order to emerge as independent adults, no longer needing their protection. But, unfortunately, this process leaves us feeling guilty because we've had to kill off the good parts of our parents as well as the bad parts in order to become independent. I imagine Sherry feeling invisible, feeling taken for granted and screaming at her parents in their separate houses, 'I hate you! I hate everything about you!' Having screamed these things, she then has to pretend that she meant every word. She has to act like a fully grown adult, invulnerable and immoveable. To keep up the pretence, she has to kill off the child within her, the 'pathetic attention seeker' who once liked drama. Our task in counselling will be to reintegrate that enthusiastic little girl as an important part of Sherry, enriching rather than disabling her.

I ask her what she was like when she was small.

'Don't know. I wasn't like I am now, that's for sure! I was a daddy's girl for a start! I was always wanting to do things with him. I was his favourite – you could tell...'

'And then?'

'Don't know. It just sort of changed. He was away a lot. I was busy at school. Him and mum were arguing all the time, so I used to go to my room and do drawings.'

'Drawings of…?'

'Imaginary things… Places to go, lakes and the seaside and stuff like that. Stupid, really.'

'They sound like good places.'

She smiles slightly. 'They were. But it was kids' stuff. When we moved house, I chucked all the drawings in the bin.'

I wince. It's easy to see why cynical-Sherry-the-teenager emerged to protect hurt-Sherry-the-child. We go on with our talking, trying to recognise the hurt child without embarrassing the cynical teenager, allowing Sherry to keep her cynical defences if she needs them, while acknowledging that there's more to her than meets the eye: her defences are only doing a job, protecting her, as I'm sure her grandmother knows.

Like the relationships we create with counsellors, the ones we create with grandparents (usually) prove that we're not such bad sons and daughters after all. I imagine that when she's with her grandmother, cynical-Sherry-the-teenager can relax and breathe, knowing that she's not – after all – the bad, hating daughter she pretended to be when she was saying all those things to her parents. Grandparents provide opportunities to make amends. They also provide opportunities to think about death because, alive or dead, grandparents come to represent a particular perspective on life – usually that life is short and it's best to get on with it while you can. Grandparents get frail. They get ill. Their deaths help prepare us for the deaths of our parents and, ultimately, for our own deaths. Sometimes a grandparent is dying or dead and I talk explicitly with the young person about what happened – about how other people reacted, about what the young person felt and wished and regretted and was glad about. A grandparent's funeral may be the first funeral that the young person has ever attended.

In 'The Old Fools', Larkin's (2003) meditation on ageing, he reminds us that 'At death, you break up' (l.13). This is precisely young people's anxiety: after thirteen or more years of piecing and holding together a sense of self, resisting extinction and annihilation, young people look ahead to old age and to the very thing they've worked so hard to resist – breaking up.

6

ATTACHMENT AND DEATH

Lacy's been cutting herself and feeling suicidal. She hasn't seen her drug-addicted father for years and her relationship with her mother has become more and more chaotic. When we meet for the first time, she tells me the family story and I encourage her to say more, especially about her parents, imagining that her distress will have its roots in these earliest, formative relationships.

But she doesn't want to talk about these. Instead, she wants to talk about her boyfriend. She loves him to bits, she says. He's everything to her. He makes her *so* happy and yet she's petrified of losing him – particularly to other girls. Because of this, she worries all the time: worries that she's too fat, too boring, too young, not good enough in bed. And to make up for these deficiencies, she does everything she can to keep him – washing his clothes, tidying his bedroom, cleaning his mother's house, cooking for him – everything! When this makes no difference and the threat of losing him still seems as great as ever, that's when she despairs, that's when she cuts and feels like killing herself.

Like most young people, she's known relatives who've died, but they don't concern her. Her real fear is of the death of her relationship with her boyfriend because that would feel as if she herself had died. 'If I lose him, then that's everything! My life won't be worth living. I'll probably kill myself,' she says.

She's not trying to impress me.

Fromm (1963) suggests that an awareness of our separateness from other people is 'the source of all anxiety'. I imagine that the prospect of losing this idealised boyfriend is an unconscious reminder of earlier losses in Lacy's life and, in particular, of the loss of her father. She experiences the loss of these relationships as akin to deaths because, as I described in the last chapter, they're 'selfobjects' (Kohut 1971) – extensions of Lacy herself. Like anyone, her earliest sense of herself will have developed by absorbing key relationships. When any of these relationships (with her father, for instance) is lost, she's left feeling incomplete, exposed, in danger and looking to replace that relationship, that part of herself, as quickly as possible in order to survive. For young people, finding a replacement often *does* feel like a matter of survival. Lacy may have replaced one originally ambivalent attachment (Bowlby 1969, 1973, 1980) to her father with a boyfriend to whom she's also now ambivalently attached, clinging to him and caring for him while hoping that he'll care for her. However ambivalent the quality of their relationship, to be without him now would be like losing a part of herself all over again: *it would feel like dying.*

'When I'm not with him, I don't know what he's doing! For all I know, he could be seeing other girls!'

She tells me about a row at the weekend which began when her boyfriend criticised her for being too 'clingy'.

'But how am I supposed to be?' she asks. 'He knows how much he means to me!'

At the height of the row, her boyfriend left the house and Lacy – alone in the bedroom – cut her wrist.

'I'll have that scar for the rest of my life!'

Yalom (1980) writes that 'Anxiety is always ameliorated by becoming attached to a specific object or situation' (p.189). Young people will therefore fight with everything they've got when something they prize is in danger of being taken away from them. It would be futile to suggest that Lacy's reliance on this particular boyfriend is unsustainable or out of proportion or that she should prioritise her own needs more. Her anxiety is too powerful to take account of rational suggestions like these. In any case, she probably has her own voice telling her these things and yet that voice makes no difference whatsoever. 'He's my life!' she insists.

Over the weeks, our relationship settles. She stops cutting but is still often in tears when we meet, still feeling that she's about to be deserted by her boyfriend and that there's nothing she can do about it. Somehow we have to dare to look into the void, into the possibility of a world without him, not least because I'm sure that the novelty for her boyfriend of having, in Lacy, a full-time servant desperate to do his bidding will wear off eventually. She and I have to look at the future together and get used to it – not with petrified baby-eyes but with the eyes of a fourteen-year-old girl learning to bear unhappiness without panicking.

One day I take the plunge. 'I wonder what would happen if he left you?'

'Don't say that!' she says. 'I don't even want to think about it!'

'I know you don't and hopefully it'll never happen,' I say, 'but what if it did?'

She looks blank. 'I don't know… I'd give up.'

'Give up because…?'

'Because I'd have nothing.'

'No one to love? No one to love you?'

She nods.

'And life would feel pointless…?'

She nods again.

This is the void we have to keep looking into together, the void she sees when she's on her own and when everything seems hopeless. My thinking is that if we can look into it *together*, then it loses some of its power to frighten and overwhelm. If we can do this, then her original family experience of always feeling potentially unloved and unlovable – an experience re-stimulated by the constant possibility of her boyfriend's departure – becomes a little more bearable and Lacy's inclination to kill off its power by killing off *herself* lessens.

We meet regularly and keep talking, anticipating life without him. Her anxieties remain but they're intermittent now and she no longer talks of killing herself. Clearly, the security of our relationship is becoming more and more important, and I worry about the effect on Lacy if – for some reason – I were suddenly to stop meeting with her. Because of this, we book our meetings months in advance so that she knows that no one can steal them from her and she doesn't have to be in any kind of crisis to be deserving of my time.

Attachment anxiety is always an expression of death anxiety. As I've said, *who we are* in Kohutian terms is a collection of internalised relationships – some secure and loving, others insecure and unloving. We get our resilience or otherwise through the quality of our attachments, and so the loss of an attached relationship disturbs us as if part of ourselves has been lost, has died. Perhaps what young people like Lacy experience as they live with the prospect of losing a boyfriend is a version of Kubler-Ross's (1969) five famous stages of grief in response to death: denial ('It can't happen!'), anger ('How could he do this!'), bargaining ('If only I could be a better girlfriend!'), depression ('Nothing I do makes any difference!') and acceptance.

Eventually, Lacy does come to accept the ending of her relationship with her boyfriend. After we've been meeting for a long time, daring to talk about the possibility of it ending and daring to imagine a life after the event, she comes in one day and announces that they've split up.

'And I'm glad, really,' she says matter-of-factly. 'It's funny, I don't feel that upset. In fact, it was me who suggested it!'

Whether the theorists describe us as being born attachment-seeking (Bowlby 1969) or object-seeking (Klein 1975) in order to survive, it's as if our first and most urgent awareness is of the possibility of death. This awareness quickly gets sublimated. As children, we don't spend our lives forever complaining about death or asking our parents to protect us from death. The anxiety is held in our unconscious minds and expressed obliquely through our behaviour. I've described elsewhere (Luxmoore 2010) the many ways in which young people end counselling relationships – not with the great pangs of existential despair expected of them by well-trained therapists but pragmatically, incidentally, apologetically. In my experience, their unconscious anxiety about death is more evident in the ways in which they start or are *born into* counselling relationships because to start is to commit, to invest, to believe and trust in something that will one day – by definition – end. I think Lacy was partly in despair when we started meeting – crying all the time and talking of suicide – because the prospect of starting a new relationship with me filled her with anxiety and dread, knowing that one day it would end like everything else.

Given this, young people start counselling in different ways. Alex comes in, sits down and immediately starts telling me his life story, trusting me with all sorts of important information. Although we've never met before and although, like so many young people, his story is full of losses, he's clearly desperate to attach. He's experienced plenty of things in his life which make it clear that nothing lasts forever and yet his response seems to be to attach as quickly and recklessly as possible. I seem to have become the perfect counsellor in his eyes: the only one who understands him; the only one who can save him from the world.

But, within weeks, it's come to nothing and I'm off my pedestal. He complains of having nothing left to say. He thinks he should end counselling. I try to persuade him to continue, even though our meetings will end at some point in the future. But he insists on ending *now* and, in the months that follow, seems happier with our light-hearted corridor conversations as we stop to chat between lessons. It's as if he's still keen to keep the relationship going but is wary of attaching too much and then – as he imagines – getting hurt once the relationship ends. I think this represents a kind of progress. I'm no longer idealised but nor am I demonised. We still speak, but Alex has a more realistic sense of what I can and can't be for him.

One way of defending against the anxiety of death is to merge completely with someone or something else, like Lacy merging with her boyfriend and Alex merging with me initially. Subsumed in a close relationship or enmeshed in an organisation, we then feel less isolated because our fate seems inextricably linked with that of other people. For heroic boys (see Chapter 3), determined to be independent, escaping from their mothers and rushing off into the maelstrom of life, this poses an anxious dilemma. How can

I be heroically separate, courageous in the face of death, but also connected to other people and so shielded from death? How can I merge safely without losing my precious individuality? In a sense, Alex goes from complete merger to complete separation to a more tentative, mixed relationship out of which interesting things might emerge in the future.

Gruff and suspicious, Morrison comes in for his first counselling appointment and we struggle to get started. I find myself wondering, 'If you really don't want to be here, Morrison, then why come?' Over the next few weeks, I learn that, like Alex, he also has a story full of losses which have made him wary of ever attaching to anyone or anything. Why bother, when anything good always gets taken away? Why invest in meetings with a counsellor that might even go on for a couple of years but will be bound to end, just like everything else? I could offer him this idea, trying to make conscious what's probably unconscious in Morrison, helping him better to understand his anxiety and perhaps assuaging it in the process. But I don't do this because I think it'll embarrass him, making our relationship more explicitly personal than he's prepared to admit. As far as Morrison is concerned, he meets once a fortnight with some 'counsellor bloke' (me) who's 'all right' and with whom he talks about 'stuff'... That's the way he frames it and keeps it safe. To suggest that he trusts me or likes me or that we matter to each other in any way would feel too personal. What helps is that I understand something of his anxiety about attachment and don't mind. I'm happy for the attachment between us to remain implicit rather than explicit. I *don't* need to confront him with his anxiety, trusting that in due course we'll be able to talk about whatever mixed feelings he has about our relationship.

Some young people like Morrison are ambivalent. Others like Alex rush into a counselling room, trying to attach immediately. Others still would never darken the door of anything called 'counselling' because of its potential for intimacy and dependency. All three kinds of young people are well aware of their potential isolation, their vulnerability in the face of death; they just defend themselves in different ways.

Groups can be similarly defensive. From the moment they form, all time-limited groups are aware of and working on their eventual demise. 'Is it really worth investing in this group when one day my relationship with it will end?' Groups often begin by claiming that everything's fine and everyone's happy in the group because they're still defending fiercely against the prospect of the group's death. These defences change once group members start to matter to each other. Then the prospect of losing people who actually matter begins to hit home and, over time, Kubler-Ross's (1969) processes of denial ('It's no big deal!'), anger ('Why do we have to end?'), bargaining ('Couldn't we go on a bit longer?'), depression ('What's the point?') and acceptance kick in.

Like babies desperate to survive, young people are desperate for close relationships, but those relationships make them vulnerable because they must end at some point. When Annaliese was six, her mother was badly injured in a skiing accident. Nine years later, her mother still hasn't fully recovered: her brain damaged, her speech slurred. And Annaliese is getting into terrible trouble in and out of school, her life seemingly falling to bits as she wilfully destroys everything put in place to support her. Teachers have done their very best to help but they're exasperated – hurt by her rejection of their help though mostly wise enough to know that this is Annaliese's internal world externalised and enacted at their expense.

Like them, I feel sorry for her. It would undoubtedly have been simpler if her mother had died because, since the accident, Annaliese has had to live with a physical, breathing mother who looks the same as she always did but is no longer the same: her personality has changed. I think Annaliese tries to kill off the idea of her mother every time she sabotages another potentially supportive relationship. She then revives the idea of her mother when she can't go through with the murder.

I try my best not to let her sabotage our relationship, such as it is. One week she's friendly, the next she's hostile. It's as if she's caught in a double bind, trying to kill off our relationship yet wanting it to continue; as if she's saying, 'I want you and I don't want you.' There are times when she can't live at home because she's fallen out so badly with her mother ('That bitch!') and there are times when she's back at home, settled for the time being, loyal and fiercely protective towards her mother.

In counselling, we discuss the idea of the mother she once had and the mother she has now. This is a perfectly sensible idea for her to be thinking about but it's only an idea: the emotional reality is much harder to bear. How can someone be dead but not dead, different but the same? All we can do for her as professionals is to bear her rejection of us and hope that she doesn't do anything so extreme that she forces the school to kill off its relationship with her as she rages against its imperfections, its allegedly broken promises, the many ways in which it continues to disappoint her.

'This is the parent you've got,' we might be saying to her, in effect.

'Yes, but not the parent I want!' she might retort, slamming the door behind her before calling back in a more conciliatory voice, 'See you tomorrow!'

Faced with situations like this and unable to contain their confusion, there are young people like Annaliese who externalise their upset, turning their feelings into behaviour of one dramatic kind or another, while there are other young people like Branwen who internalise their feelings.

Branwen's mother hasn't been in an accident but has developed a mental illness which comes and goes. 'It's like she's not my mum any more,' says Branwen.

It's hard to underestimate the difficulty of this for Branwen and her younger brother. It's as if their mother – the one they know and love and who loves them – dies and then comes back to life and then dies again. This keeps happening. Branwen has no way of knowing how long it'll go on for and whether things will ever get back to normal.

Outwardly, she remains calm and composed, but inside she's very, very sad. She starts stealing and admits that this is partly to make her parents angry because she can't be angry with them herself. She becomes obsessive about her bedroom, agreeing with me that this is a way of keeping control when so many other things in her life are out of control. Through all this, I keep assuring her that the situation at home really *is* difficult and really *is* unfair. I keep admitting to her that there's no easy way out. And I keep reminding myself that she's still a fifteen-year-old girl with normal fifteen-year-old things to worry about like friends and school and how she looks. We discuss as many of these things as possible in between our conversations about her mother.

Over the months, nothing changes. Her mother's illness comes and goes. I keep Branwen company. She's absorbing a powerful message about life's unpredictability and about the transience of relationships. When she tells me one day about a nice boy and tells me that she's started going out with him, I'm delighted because, despite knowing that nothing lasts forever, she's still prepared to invest in this relationship: in other words, she's still a fifteen-year-old girl doing fifteen-year-old things. When she tells me a few weeks later that she might be pregnant, I'm perturbed and quickly arrange for her to see a doctor. Yet being pregnant makes a kind of sense because – living with the loss of her own mother ('It's like she's not my mum any more') – it's as if Branwen is setting about becoming a mother herself to make up for that loss. She's creating new life, attaching and merging with her baby and, in so doing, feeling less alone. Whether or not this happens to be the best thing to be doing at this stage of her life, it still makes sense.

She learns from the doctor that she's not pregnant after all and doesn't seem to mind, perhaps scared at the thought of having a baby but at the same time reassured to know that she *could* get pregnant, *could* be a mother if she chose.

Living with all sorts of losses, young people merge and separate, attach and detach… One day, a few weeks before their exams start and not long before they're due to leave school, I happen to have sessions with three different girls. By coincidence, each girl spends her session telling me about a friend with whom she's recently fallen out – a friend since childhood, a really good friend. Each of the three is adamant that there's no going back. The die is cast. That particular friendship is now ended. Forever.

Talking about her best friend, one girl says, 'If she thinks I'm going to apologise after being friends all these years, then she's got another think coming!'

Another girl is talking about a friend who always holidayed with the family: 'I never thought she'd do anything like this! To be honest, I don't know what I ever saw in her!'

'She can fuck herself!' says the third girl about a friend from whom she was once inseparable. 'It's sad that this has happened. But if that's how she wants it, then fuck her!'

Of course, friendships change and close friendships sometimes implode when they become claustrophobic. But I can't help thinking that this is too much of a coincidence: on the same day, three unconnected girls are all telling me about the break-up of old friendships just as the three of them are about to leave school. And each of the girls paints herself as blameless, done unto, betrayed by a disloyal and uncaring friend.

It may sound odd but I think that the three girls are practising for the day when they leave school, unconsciously preparing themselves for that rupture, that separation, that loss as they leave school and start a period of uncertainty when their relationship with the external world will – at the very least – be different. I think they're practising for what it'll be like to feel bereft, abandoned, cast out and unable to turn back the clock. I think they're mourning the loss of their lives so far. As Frankel (1998) writes, 'Thoughts, feelings, and insights into the nature of human mortality arise because adolescents are undergoing, at an experiential level, a death and dying process' (p.120).

Maybe this is what young people do when they deliberately break up with friends. Maybe at some level they're always checking to see whether they can survive the aloneness, daring themselves to move on without the person who once seemed so necessary. Leaving school in a few weeks means that there will no longer be ready-made friendships with which to merge and escape the anxieties of aloneness. These anxieties will have to be confronted and so it makes sense for the girls to be practising.

In the school where I work, I manage a team of students called 'peer supporters' (Luxmoore 2000, 2002) whose job in their last year at school is to befriend and support younger students – not by targeting the most needy but simply by getting to know as many students as possible in a variety of structured and unstructured ways.

As a team, we spend much of the second half of the year discussing the ending of their relationships with the many students who will have attached themselves to the team. I explain that many of these younger students will have had bad experiences of endings in their lives: of parents separating without warning because it was thought to be kinder that way; of dying relatives who were never discussed; of funerals avoided... It's kinder and more respectful to give students lots of warning about this ending, I say to the peer supporters. This way, the students can get used to the idea. They can be angry or indifferent or sad or all of these things at different times over the next few months. And this matters because we're only able to move on from our attachments once we've said a proper goodbye.

The peer supporters are sceptical about all this psycho-theory. 'To be honest, I don't think they're that bothered!' they tell me. 'Or at least none of them seemed particularly interested last week when I told them I was leaving...' Other peer supporters claim to have forgotten to say anything about leaving but will admit that the real reason they've 'forgotten' is because they can't bear to bring up the subject. So I insist, and, reluctantly, they do eventually find a way of filtering it into their conversations. Sometimes they make full-scale announcements to classes. But, right up to the end, there's still a degree of scepticism in the team about my apparent obsession with endings.

Only at the very last does it make sense. On their final day, there's a farewell assembly. The peer supporters are given presents. Younger students cry. They hug the peer supporters and don't want to let go. Tributes are paid. There's more hugging. One or two peer supporters find themselves crying. All admit to being moved and not a little surprised.

'I didn't realise I meant so much to them!' says one peer supporter. 'They seemed to be really sad about it. Even the boys!'

'Especially the boys!' says another.

Because of their squeamishness about expressing certain feelings, boys are often assumed to be unfeeling little sociopaths. As I've written elsewhere (Luxmoore 2000), they get a bad press. I'm extremely sympathetic to their difficulties but, even so, I really struggle with Simon. He smiles rarely. A flicker here and there. An occasional acknowledgement of something I might have said. Then back to it…

'I'm thinking of getting this new game!'

I struggle because it's hard to get him to talk about anything other than computer games. I try to be patient because I think that talking about computer games is his way of making a relationship with me and of re-establishing that relationship at the start of every session, the way other young people might start by talking about the weather or about football or about whatever happened on television last night. So I'm patient but I'm always looking for opportunities to get him talking about his family, which is where I think his anxieties really lie.

Always we come back to computer games, computer games… To be fair, other young people have 'things' that fill their lives and about which they talk equally passionately. In the run-up to Christmas, they list the many expensive, unnecessary things they're going to be given by guilty-sounding parents and step-parents and, during the rest of the year, they're forever describing new things they want and will usually be given. Yet they're coming to see me because of how they *feel*, I keep reminding myself – not because of needing to list their possessions.

One way of understanding these conversations is that the 'things' they talk about are transitional objects (Winnicott 1971), no longer the teddy bears or bits of mouldy blanket beloved of small children, the keepsakes easing a child's transition from its mother to a world of more varied relationships. The 'things' preoccupying young people like Simon might represent ways of staying safe in the same way that teddy bears or bits of blanket might help younger children to feel safe. Some of these teenage 'things' are desired just as fervently as a baby might desire a nipple. They might be clothes, bikes, audio equipment or, in Simon's case, computer games. They might be phones – better designed and more complex than ever before. Whenever a teacher tries to confiscate a phone or some other important 'thing', a verbal and sometimes physical tussle ensues because it feels to the young person as if a part of him or herself is being removed. 'My phone is my life!' one girl said to me. 'Without my phone, I've got nothing!' Phones are the gateways to hundreds of relationships. Phones represent attachments. Young people check their phones as often as a child checks to see that its mother's still there because, as long as that young person is in contact with other people, he or she feels safe.

Transitional objects or not, still I'm stuck with Simon talking endlessly about his computer games (interactive, a bit like a phone) and I'm still trying to shift him on to talking about other things. Still I'm trying to be patient but actually I'm very bored.

Then one day he comes in and it's all different. This time he talks about how low he's feeling, how miserable and friendless. Suddenly, it's as if the computer-games gambit has failed and all his underlying feelings come tumbling out. And they're feelings about *people* – about people not liking him, about people not wanting to meet up with him, about people trying to boss him about. At last we're in business and it occurs to me that all along I could have been asking what it would be like *not* to have the games. I could have been asking about what that would feel like, about what exactly he'd be missing. Then we might have got on to this underlying stuff sooner.

At some level, our materialism is always a response to death. We attach to 'things' because they're solid and because we can control them more easily than we can control people who are changeable and capable of disappearing or dying. There's a real desperation about Simon's enthusiasm for things. He won't be deflected from talking about his games, as if he's clinging to them, endlessly arranging and rearranging them in his mind; as if he's thinking, 'If only I can control my games, I'll be able to control my life.'

'Things' take the place of human relationships. Parents pacify their children with things like food and sweets and, when the children are older, fob them off with bigger and better and more things. Some young people end up unable to talk about relationships and only able to talk about things. They get older and substitute the buzz of alcohol or drugs for the buzz of food or sweets or computer games.

'Things' keep at bay a particular panic because they can be controlled. But what if all our accumulated possessions amount to nothing? What then? What happens to us? What if, ultimately, we must make relationships with *people* to feel safe? And what if we can't control people the way that we can control 'things'?

Unable to sustain the computer games conversation any longer, Simon's feelings overwhelm him. 'I don't know,' he says, looking at the ground. 'I'm feeling really bad. Like I've got no friends.'

I ask what's happened.

'Nothing, really. I'm just feeling bad. Like nobody really likes me. They pretend they do when they want something but they're not my friends really. If they were my friends, they wouldn't be like they are.'

'Which is what?'

'I don't know,' he says, head bowed. 'I don't know.'

'Like teasing you? Ignoring you? Laughing at you?'

This is too much to admit. 'Not really. Not really teasing. Just being annoying!'

'And that gets you down...?'

He says nothing.

'People *can* be really annoying,' I say.

He makes a face as if to say that this is the understatement of the century.

'They can be really annoying sometimes and they can be really good friends sometimes. Sometimes they're both!'

He squirms, saying nothing, letting me finish.

'I wonder sometimes if they're annoying because we really like them and then they let us down?'

He says nothing. If we're beginning to work on the possibility of Simon feeling ambivalently about people, then we've probably gone as far as we can go for today. As far as he can bear to go.

'Anyway,' he says, looking up, animated again, 'I'm thinking of getting this new game...'

7

UNPROTECTED SEX

It's New Year's Eve and young people are gathering, full of expectation. More than at any other time of the year, this particular evening seems to mark the physical passing of time. After midnight, we'll suddenly be a year older; we'll say goodbye to the old year and look ahead...to what exactly? The crowds swell, young people in particular getting more and more exuberant, until, at last, the clock strikes twelve and, frantically, they start hugging and kissing each other.

Officially this is called 'celebrating the new year', but I think that the excitement of New Year's Eve is also an expression of collective anxiety: an anxiety about time passing, about not knowing what the future will hold or what will become of us. Adults turn to each other and ask, 'I wonder what we'll be doing in a year's time?' while thinking to themselves, 'I wonder who'll have died?' They begin to disperse, but the young people in the crowd are still shouting and dashing around as if to prove that they, at least, will live forever.

New Year's Eve may provide an obvious focus for everyone's anxieties, but something similar happens amongst young people at weekends during the rest of the year...

Rhona is full of scorn for the girls younger than herself who go out on Friday and Saturday nights to get drunk and have sex. 'They're pathetic!' she says. 'They don't realise how stupid they look when they're falling down pissed and letting boys do stuff...' Yet she herself was part of the Friday and Saturday night scene less than a year ago. The difference now is that she has a regular boyfriend and opportunities to stay indoors with him. This has changed everything: she's calmer, has begun to work harder at school and is even talking about staying on at school after she's sixteen.

She tells me that the Friday and Saturday night girls are scornful of the fact that she and her boyfriend use condoms.

'They say condoms are stupid and it's better without! Can you believe that?'

We look at each other – aghast – and I'm dismayed. How could they possibly think that? They know perfectly well what happens if they don't use condoms! This is the very opposite of everything that they've been taught!

Rhona agrees.

So I find myself wondering. These young people aren't stupid. Okay, they get drunk – ridiculously drunk – and drunk people make mistakes – but, even so, why would they *deliberately* take the risk of not using a condom? Once upon a time it would have been simply a matter of ignorance and male irresponsibility and, of course, these problems persist. But young people are much better informed nowadays and have much better access to contraception. I wonder how much the recklessness of getting drunk and, in particular, the recklessness of unprotected sex represents a curiosity about all the things in life over which young people have no control, all the things that can go wrong. Like watching the clock relentlessly tick its way to midnight on New Year's Eve, it's as if there's something exciting and compulsive about playing the lotteries of pregnancy and sexually transmitted infection. 'Will I get caught this time or will I escape? What would it be like to live my life uncontrolled, *unprotected* by anyone or anything?' If death is the great authority figure, the big clock always in control (see Chapter 4), then how much are young people on Friday and Saturday nights taking their lives into their own hands and daring that great authority figure to do its worst? Yalom (1980) describes sex as 'death defeating' because 'Death is connected with banality and ordinariness' (p.194) whereas sex is exciting and magical. He notes that there's often an increase in the sexual activity of people diagnosed with life-threatening illnesses and that, for these people, their behaviour is a 'repression of death anxiety' (p.382). Perhaps, as they grow up, young people start to realise that they have a life-threatening condition called mortality and, for some, sex is a way of responding to that realisation, a way of merging anxiously with another person so as not to be alone. Interestingly, young people are usually the first to be touched by the thought of any animal species threatened with extinction: immediately they start writing letters, campaigning, protesting. Perhaps on Friday and Saturday nights they flirt with the physical power of conception as a way of protesting against their own extinction.

I think there's unconscious method in the madness of Friday and Saturday nights. Sex and death focus our most physical and most philosophical anxieties and yet conversations about sex and death are usually discouraged by polite society. Young people are encouraged to delay sex and not think about death. Plenty of time for that in the future! So, anxiously, they rush into sex as they rush into life, experimenting, trying everything before it's too late. I wonder how much a tendency to start sexual relationships earlier and earlier is related, in part, to a tendency to deny death more and more determinedly. I wonder how much young people explore sex as a way of searching for meaning and purpose in their lives and as a way of convincing themselves that they'll never die. Sex might be a way of feeling especially alive.

I remember a tutor at university saying that all literature was ultimately about sex and death, and I think he was right. The French refer to orgasm as 'la petite mort' and 'dying' was Elizabethan slang for orgasm. Young people are forever *dying* to know, *dying* for a fag, a dump, a drink, a shag, a joint…'dying' always for some kind of relief. Perhaps orgasm is a reminder that the body is capable of usurping the mind, a reminder of what Becker (1973) calls 'our animal fate', of the fact that we are 'gods with anuses' (p.51). When young people are supposed to be learning to control their bodies with their minds, perhaps sex and, to a lesser extent, drug taking become ways of exploring of what it's like to lose control, regressing to a childlike state, postponing adulthood and the implications of adulthood.

Sex might be one way in which young people like the Friday-and-Saturday-night brigade defy all that death represents. But sex can also be a surrendering, a giving up. Letting life do its worst ('Fuck it! I don't care!') might be a defiant attitude for some, but not for Baylie. For weeks we've talked about her mother and father hating each other: her mother depressed and unable to look after Baylie; her father angry, unable to understand or forgive his daughter's behaviour. When I say something about her parents' own needs getting in the way of loving their daughter, Baylie merely shrugs.

'Doesn't matter,' she says, as if to reassure me. 'Fuck them! I don't need them anyway. I've got my friends.'

She's part of the Friday-and-Saturday-night brigade. I hear from other young people that Baylie will let anyone have sex with her. 'She's got no self-respect,' they say. 'She doesn't realise that boys are only using her.'

But she realises full well. 'I know they're only after one thing,' she says. 'But it doesn't bother me. I let them. Doesn't do any harm, does it! It's only sex!'

The way in which we express ourselves sexually says a lot about our sense of ourselves and sense of other people. It speaks of our neediness, of our ability to negotiate and share, to achieve and delay gratification. It speaks of our relationship with control and abandon. So, with young people, sex might be cautious and sanitised; it might be brutal and uncaring; it might be passive and powerless. Mechanical, unloving sex might be proof for Baylie that life is mechanical and unloving, a purely physical exchange between two people. If tenderness and attachment are too elusive or too painful to bear, then better not be tender, better not attach. Just fuck.

When I ask if the boys use condoms, she looks sheepish.

'I know what you're going to say! I know, I know! But sometimes you just get carried away!' She makes it sound as if the sex gets so passionate that she and her boyfriends are transported to a higher place, miles away from some damp shed where an older boy, grunting, jabs his penis into Baylie and warns her not to tell anyone.

Hers is a what-the-fuck surrender to life and death. 'What the fuck does it matter? If no one cares, then what do I care? It's just sex! So what if people call me a whore? See if I care!' Her surrender is just as dangerous as another young person's defiance because, in feeling that she has nothing to lose, Baylie risks everything. And yet hers is also a searching for someone else's undivided attention, for the thrill of being desired, of existing (however briefly) in the eyes of another person, no longer alone.

I decide to describe her choices as explicitly and as matter-of-factly as possible. 'So you're saying that you let boys have sex with you and you know they don't love you and you're not bothered whether or not they use a condom...'

She winces. 'Sounds bad, doesn't it!'

'No, it's really clear. It's what you've decided. It's you making a choice for yourself.'

'But that's bad, isn't it?'

'I think it's what you've chosen and I think you've got your reasons. One reason might be feeling that if no one cares about you, then why should you care about yourself?'

She nods, pleased that I've understood.

'Another reason might be that you like sex!'

'Yeah!' she laughs, twisting a strand of hair between her finger and thumb. 'Only I don't always. I don't like it when boys want you to do stuff that's gross.'

'But it's hard to say no when they call you names?'

She makes a scornful face. 'That sort of thing...'

'So you go along with it but wish you didn't have to, because it feels like not having a choice?'

'No,' she corrects me, 'I do have a choice. It's my life, isn't it?'

I agree with her. 'It *is* your life and at the end of the day no one can make you do anything. You have control... Control is good, but control is scary.'

She's drifting away. I ask what she's thinking.

'Sorry! I was just thinking about this boy. You don't know him. He thinks he's such a big man because he's got a car. Thinks he can have me whenever he wants...'

She continues the story, her indignation rising. I say nothing. Sometimes making the existential situation clear ('You have choice, but choice is scary') offers young people a reality they've been avoiding. That reality is less personal than they've been choosing to believe: no one is persecuting *or* protecting them; in fact, they're on their own. Ours isn't a moralising conversation between Baylie and a concerned counsellor urging her to be more careful. Rather, it's an amoral statement of fact, a bald description of her aloneness and power. I have to wait and see what happens. If her life crashes further, then, with other professionals, I'll do my best to support her. But sometimes young people get into more and more trouble in order to get more and more support: they avoid the very independence they claim to want, where 'Just leave me alone!' really means 'Please don't leave me alone!' Responding to Baylie's every dependent whim does no more good than berating her every mistake. I think it's important to be clear with her about the big existential questions, approaching them with no ready-made answers and with no bullshit (as young people would say) because these are the big questions fuelling any young person's behaviour... 'What's the point of my life? Why do I feel so lonely? Who will love me?' Hobson (1985) distinguishes between two modes of loneliness – 'no-being' and 'cut-offness'. Although we haven't articulated it, I sense that Baylie has times when she feels as if she doesn't really exist ('no-being') or might as well not exist if no one desires her. She certainly has times when she cuts herself off from feelings and relationships. Hobson argues that because loneliness is inarticulate, the task of psychotherapy is to 'penetrate to the core of loneliness in each person and speak to that' (p.268). Acknowledging the depths of a young person's despair doesn't magically change that young person's life but sometimes it brings the young person back from the brink of loneliness. It connects.

If Baylie's sexual relationships say something about her view of herself as unlovable and powerless, Anita's relationships are ways in which she punishes herself. She's fourteen. Every Friday and Saturday night, she goes out and gets drunk. Usually, she ends up having sex with someone.

'My family say they don't know what's the matter with me and, to be honest, I don't know either. I don't know why I do it. I hate myself for what I've become.'

Listening to her story, I suggest to her that her behaviour makes absolute sense. Last year her mother got ill and, three months later, died. During those months, Anita refused to visit the hospital. Then, when her mother died, she couldn't tear herself away from the body lying in the chapel-of-rest.

She agrees that she feels guilty about not visiting.

'Maybe,' I suggest, 'as well as loving your mother and feeling protective towards her and sorry for her and close to her – all of which things are true... Maybe there's also a part of you that hated her for being ill?'

She nods.

'And hated her for dying?'

She nods again.

'She wasn't supposed to get ill. She was supposed to be your mother. She wasn't supposed to get ill and die.'

Anita agrees.

'So maybe you hate yourself at the moment because if you hated your mother it would make the guilty feeling worse? Maybe you act like you're having fun on Friday and Saturday nights but maybe you're punishing yourself, Anita? Taking it out on yourself?'

She thinks about this.

'Maybe the truth is that you loved her so much that you can't bear to be without her...'

Tears well in her eyes.

'You were her loving daughter and always will be. Whether you punish yourself for the rest of your life for not being perfect is up to you.'

Brody isn't part of the Friday-and-Saturday-night scene. He's older and more sophisticated. He comes to see me, hair immaculate and t-shirt stretched tight to show off his muscles. He says he keeps having one-night stands and can't understand why. As soon as the sex is over, he's no longer interested and the girl is left confused and upset. 'I don't know what's the matter with me! I've got this really bad reputation. Some weekends I have two or three different girls!'

I don't know whether to be impressed by his sexual prowess or by his honesty in coming to talk about it. I also have a vague sense that I'm being charmed. Eventually, I ask about his earlier life, but he's reluctant to look at anything to do with family relationships. I get the feeling that I'm not giving him the answers he wants, but at the end of the session I suggest that it would be good to meet again.

Politely, he declines, thanking me anyway.

I'm disappointed because we've barely scratched the surface. Then, as I'm writing up my notes afterwards, it dawns on me that he's just had a one-night stand with me, in effect. As the girls probably feel, I've been left feeling as if I wasn't good enough, as if I've disappointed him. I curse myself because, had I realised sooner, I could have pointed out what was happening between us. Rarely do I risk making here-and-now interpretations with young people because the power imbalance and risk of unfairly exposing the young person are too great. But on this occasion the insight might have helped Brody think about what was making it difficult for him to meet with me for a second time and, by extension, what was making it difficult for him to stay with any of the girls. It's as if he's looking to them (and to me) for answers to unspoken questions: 'Why do I feel so alone? Will I always be alone? How can I stop feeling alone? If – like sex – everything always ends and we're alone again, then what's the point?'

Roach's relationships with girls are also short-term. He says he wants to understand why he loses interest as soon as he starts going out with a girl. Is there something wrong with him?

This time, I sense that I'm being trusted rather than charmed. Although Roach's inclination is to rationalise away any feelings that threaten to surface and although, in his way, he's just as defended and just as isolated as Brody, the difference between them is that Roach is keen to come back for more sessions. Yalom (1980) argues that 'engagement is the therapist's most effective approach to meaninglessness' (p.481). We exist and have meaning only in relationship to other people (see Chapter 5). Without those relationships, without those people, we mean nothing. Roach may not be aware of it but – at least in counselling – he's experimenting with a longer relationship. As with Brody, I sense that I'm disappointing him by not coming up with the rational answers he'd like but, this time, I acknowledge my inadequacy.

He says it's fine.

I suggest that not knowing how a relationship will develop is normal; that not knowing exactly how we feel is normal. So rather than give up on something because the answer isn't obvious, we can give ourselves time and see how things progress.

'But I tried doing that with Katy!'

'I know you did. And it's all we *can* do. Either we split up or we wait and see how things go. And we try not to panic. You meet with me every week and you never know what we're going to talk about. But you wait and you see how it goes.'

'You're not my girlfriend, though!' he laughs. 'It's different!'

'Different in some ways. But we're still two people meeting and trying to connect with each other. Some days we might feel very connected. Other days we might not.'

I think that Brody and Roach are both afraid of being alone. Because of this, muscular Brody skips from girl to girl, having sex with all of them to prove that he's not alone, yet still he feels alone afterwards. Penetration might be a fleeting moment of connection, but the prospect of any enduring connection remains just as elusive for Brody as it must have felt earlier in his life when the feeling of aloneness began. My suspicion is that he can't forgive the girls for their imperfections and that sex always seems imperfect because the orgasm never lasts. After all the build-up, suddenly it's over and the disappointment kicks in. Nothing lasts. In psychoanalytical theory (Klein 1957), this is similar to the disappointment that we feel as babies and small children: disappointed by our mother's imperfections, by the fact that she's not there all the time; disappointed that our physical connection with her keeps being interrupted, that she can be so wonderful and yet at other times so awful. Brody's macho, muscular grandiosity (probably) feels as isolating for him now as it (probably) felt when he was about twelve years old, insisting that he no longer needed a mother to help him because her imperfect help was too much to bear. If she couldn't be there all the time, it felt better to be without her all the time.

Brody never comes back to see me, and, again, I suggest to Roach that I'm not giving him the answers he wants.

'That's okay,' he says. 'It's helping.'

'How's it helping?'

'I don't know,' he says. 'It just is. I'm not used to talking about stuff like this.'

Lots of young people would say the same thing. What they mean is that they've never allowed themselves to stay in a relationship where the outcome is unclear, where they know perfectly well that they're not the most important person in the other person's life, where the other person doesn't make everything all right, and yet that doesn't seem to matter: it's good enough. Aloneness and death never go away, but our fear of them is tempered by the connections we make with one another, however imperfect those connections might be.

8

COCK-UP OR CONSPIRACY

Kumar punches walls. I saw him do it as he made his way to the headteacher's office and it scared me – the force, the futility, the pain. After meeting with the headteacher, he came on to his appointment with me, hand wrapped in an ice bandage, calmer now despite having just been excluded for the rest of the day for swearing at a teacher. He'd punched walls before, he said. He'd certainly sworn at teachers.

There are more boys claiming to have punched walls or to have punched 'massive holes' in their bedroom doors than boys who've actually done it. Nevertheless, there's something about the *idea* of punching a wall that's important for young people. It seems to represent a final, absolute confrontation with all the things in life that are unfair and can't be changed. Kumar punches the corridor wall on his way to the headteacher's office and *still* he gets excluded, *still* his mother's more interested in his baby brother, *still* his father's depressed, *still* dyslexia undermines his work at school.

'Nothing good ever happens to me,' he says. 'I know I've got to look on the bright side – I know there are people worse off than me – but I can't stop thinking about it. It's always the same! It's always me who gets the crap!'

I say something about life not being fair.

'It isn't!' he says. 'It bloody isn't!'

But he's calmer. I let him continue, echoing rather than contradicting him. This is verbal wall-punching, in effect – better than actual wall-punching – and Kumar is no different from the rest of us, lashing out when the world seems to be conspiring against us. Hearing that our frustration is real rather than foolish seems to help because – however antisocial a young person's behaviour may be – the issue underlying the frustration is difficult to think about… *Why do bad things happen?*

Lizzy says she was there when the boy drowned. She and her friend Mica had been speaking to him earlier in the day and since that day she's always wondered… 'What if we'd talked to him for longer and made him late for the trip? Or what if we hadn't talked to him and he'd gone earlier? What if we'd done something, *anything*, to change what happened that morning? Then he wouldn't have drowned. Other people would have been there. Everything would have been different.'

Looking back on his youth, Michael Frayn (2010) asks the same question:

> If my mother hadn't died I shouldn't have gone to university, I know. I shouldn't have followed the career that I did follow. Shouldn't have made the friends I made. Shouldn't have met my first wife or my second. My children wouldn't exist, or my grandchildren either… (pp.184–5)

The thought that a single event can have momentous consequences is as alarming for Lizzy thinking about the boy who drowned as it is for Frayn, who goes on, 'Even to think about this possibility is to feel the world around me dissolving into black nothingness, to be seized by existential terror' (pp.184–5).

Whether directly connected or not with the boy who drowned, Lizzy's behaviour in school at the moment is all about testing her existential power. 'If I do this, what'll happen? If I do that, what'll be different? If I do nothing, what then?' She's curious about the effect of her choices and actions – probing, pushing people and situations to see what happens, what effect she has. It's as if she's playing her own kind of Russian roulette, working out the percentages and probabilities. 'If I say "crap" to a teacher, will I get into trouble? What about if I say "shit" or – worse still – "fuck"? What'll happen if I'm late for school? Or skip school? What about if I don't do my coursework? Or break friends with Mica? Or make friends with the girl nobody likes? What if I'm popular? Or unpopular?'

Because of her behaviour, she irritates everyone around her and constantly gets herself into trouble. She may be genuinely angry or sad about all sorts of things in her life but she's also exploring what Knox (2011) calls 'teleological agency': 'What degree of control do I have over my life if other people also have control?' Knox describes how our sense of emotional and psychological agency develops from a physical sense of agency: 'Infants discover themselves by exploring the reactions that they create in others in response to their own actions' (p.31). Young people's changing bodies therefore affect their sense of agency, their sense of what they can and can't do. Suddenly, they're bigger and stronger. They can have sexual intercourse. They're becoming more and more powerful, and they deal with this increased sense of agency, argues Coleman (2011), by focusing on different things at different times, spacing out their preoccupations so as not to be overwhelmed by the many things they must explore and understand. One day, their preoccupation might be school; the next day, it might be friends; the next week, parents; the week after that, siblings and so on, with parents complaining all the while that 'If it's not one thing, it's another! They're never happy! Why can't they just relax and enjoy their lives?'

Coleman identifies two kinds of agency: the agency required to make present-day choices and the agency required to make choices about the future. I would add a third kind of agency which is the agency required to develop some sense of ourselves in the greater scheme of things – a philosophical kind of agency. Lizzy may be irritating people with her daily choices; she may be getting into trouble because of the choices she's making about her future, but, all the while, she's making urgent enquiries about what happens when it comes to matters of life and death. That's why her story about the boy who drowned is important. What degree of control can human beings ever have when natural disasters occur, putting our puny lives into perspective? 'What agency can I have when it comes to a boy drowning? What part do I play? How much will the life I'm living now affect my death?' Lizzy's a heavy smoker. She knows all the dangers of smoking but can't decide whether or not to give up. Nor can she decide whether or not to work hard at school, whether or not to invest in a future affected by whatever results she gets in her exams.

'I keep starting on something and then always feel like giving up,' she says.

Keegan comes to see me because he's completely unsure about what to do when he leaves school. And leaving is imminent. Unless he makes up his mind, he'll miss out on all sorts of opportunities, including the opportunity of going to university. He's stuck, unsure what he's good at, unsure what interests him, unsure what's worth doing. We talk about the usual things: the expectations of him at home and what he feels like saying to his parents; the mixed feelings he has; the messages he's imbibed from childhood...

Nothing seems especially important until our fifth session when he's talking casually about the death of his grandmother. 'It made me realise that this is the last of everything.'

I ask what he means.

'I mean that it's the last time we'll meet on this day. It's the last time we'll have this exact conversation in this room. It's the last time I'll be exactly this old... Everything that happens is happening for the last time!'

He's right. It's as if his grandmother's death has provoked in Keegan a heightened sense of time passing and a persistent question: because life is finite and time is short, should we be frantically planning ahead, arranging our lives, or should we be trying to conserve time, relishing every second as it passes?

The context is interesting: his father has recently been made redundant from a high-powered job and admits to enjoying the unexpected time off; his mother is deciding whether or not to do the course in horticulture that she's talked about for years. 'Not because she wants to be a gardener,' Keegan says, 'but just because she's interested.'

He's trying to make a decision about his life at the same time as his parents are trying to decide what's worth doing in their lives. The snag is that neither of them talks with him about their own deliberations. Instead, they urge him simply to go to university as if there's no other decision to be made. Keegan resists their exhortations and rightly so, I think.

For many young people, there's a link between controlling life and controlling death. 'If I can control my life, then surely I'll be able to control my death? In which case – great – I'll get started! But – hang on – if I'm going to die anyway and can't possibly control that, then what's the point of trying to control my life? In fact, what's the point of anything?'

I ask Carla whether she thinks much about her brother who died while he was still a baby, the year before she was born.

She says she does wonder what it would be like if he was around today. 'I wonder what my life would be like,' she says. 'I wonder if I'd have been born. But I know that everything happens for a reason.'

'Even bad things?'

'Bad things are meant to test us.'

'And if bad things keep happening?'

She hesitates.

'You could be right,' I say, 'but what if things happen randomly? What if there's no plan? What if – as they say – shit happens and there's nothing we can do about it?'

'I suppose,' she says, 'but then what would be the point?'

'Good question!'

'There's got to be a point…'

'Has there?'

'Of course! Otherwise we wouldn't know what to do. We wouldn't care about anything. We'd be in a complete mess!'

'So we spend our lives looking for the point of being alive…?'

'Exactly!' she says. 'Well, I do anyway!'

'And what have you found so far?'

She grins. 'I knew you'd say that! I don't know, do I! It's hard!'

I agree with her. This is at the heart of young people's questioning. Why *do* things happen the way they do? Why don't we get what we deserve? Why do bad things happen to good people? Why do older brothers die before we're born? Why? Is there meaning in these things or is life quite arbitrary? To what extent can we ever control our destinies?

'Maybe there are some things we can control,' I suggest, 'and other things we can't. Maybe it's always a struggle between the two. We might spend ages planning our lives and trying to make things happen but we can never know exactly what's going to happen…'

She frowns. 'It's depressing when you think about it. Makes you feel like giving up.'

'It might sometimes.'

'Not if you believe in God, though.'

'Do you?'

'Sort of… I believe my brother's in heaven. And I believe I'll meet up with him one day.'

Originally, Carla came to see me because she couldn't stop crying. So many people had gone out of her life, she said – her father when she was young, her best friend when she was eight, another best friend when she was twelve and her boyfriend just recently. 'All the good people leave!' she said, pressing soggy tissues to her eyes. 'It's like there's something wrong with me!'

As we talked, her immediate panic subsided and that was when I learned about the brother who died before she was born. I started wondering whether her story about the many losses in her life began with that loss and with her need to understand its purpose. Was the world deliberately picking on her or was there no intelligent purpose behind any of these losses?

'I believe in heaven,' she says, 'but I don't believe in God when it comes to other things like famine and earthquakes and stuff like that, because if there's a God he wouldn't let those things happen. So I don't know, really... Some things I believe in but other things I don't.'

'And people dying? People going out of your life?'

'I don't know,' she says. 'Aren't you supposed to tell me the answer?'

We laugh.

'Those things certainly didn't happen because of anything you did, Carla!'

Freud (1923) suggests that we view death as a punishment from the superego. We believe that we must be doing something right if we're alive and must have done something very wrong if we're dead or dying because the all-seeing, hypercritical superego is clearly meting out stern justice. Of course, Freud's suggestion is only useful if it rings true as a way of understanding and articulating our experience. Do young people *really* think of death as a punishment? They're certainly attracted to the simplicity of an eye for an eye, a life for a life. They're attracted to the idea that if you do something bad, then something bad should happen to you and you'll have deserved it. They complain about things being against them and are forever wondering what they've done to deserve their latest misfortune. Perhaps their sense of deserving and not deserving comes from a sense of always being watched and judged.

'Maybe I'm jinxed,' says Carla.

'Or maybe you've had some bad luck that you haven't deserved?'

Despite not having the answers, it's helpful to wonder about these things together because it means that a young person like Carla is no longer alone with her anxieties and is therefore less likely to enact them. Mountford (2011) writes about 'aporia' – the experience of doubt, perplexity and wonder. He argues that this is often a more honest and open-minded response to life's mysteries than the strident certainties of religious fundamentalism. Himself a priest expected to provide answers, he describes theology as really a conversation rather than a set of givens, quoting the novelist Howard Jacobson's warning that 'it is not religion that is the root of all evil, it is certainty' (quoted in Mountford 2011, p.80).

Most of the young people I know express little interest in organised religion. They return from funerals with no sudden desire to start attending church or reorganising their lives along religious lines. They're curious, however, about whether there's an afterlife and about whether they'll be reunited with the person who's died. They're interested in reincarnation – joking about whether they'll come back as beautiful butterflies or slimy snakes, rewarded or punished for their lives on earth. They're interested in the idea of justice being meted out in an afterlife and, with that in mind, are interested in whether they're currently living their lives well or badly (see Chapter 9).

Her brother who died as a baby was called Carl. I ask whether Carla ever feels like a replacement, making up for the life her brother never got the chance to live.

'I used to think about that a lot,' she says. 'I used to worry that I wasn't good enough and that he'd be watching and seeing what a mess I was making of everything. I still worry about it sometimes but not so much.'

Having spent time exploring a young person's sadness or rage at the immediate circumstances of his or her life, typically we return again and again to the question 'Why do bad things happen?'

Rachel thinks it's a conspiracy. Her week's been ruined, she says, because she and her friends were supposed to be going to the leavers' ball in a limousine, but now it turns out that the limousine can only take eight people and the ninth person – Rachel – must find another way of getting herself to the ball.

'They didn't even discuss it with me!' she says indignantly. 'I was away from school on the day they found out about the limo and when I came back it had all been decided!' She hasn't spoken to her friends since finding out and apparently they've been avoiding her. 'It just shows!' she says. 'The way people stab you in the back! People who are supposed to be your friends!'

She's hurt. And this follows on from the experience that brought her to me in the first place: her father taking up with a woman barely older than Rachel and Rachel finding out about it from a friend. Again, she was hurt and furious at the thought that her father could do something like this without even telling her. We've spent weeks going over what happened and thinking about her father's life because so much hinges on this. Did her father deliberately not tell her because he didn't care or did he not tell her because somehow he never got round to it and then the news came out unexpectedly before he could sit down with Rachel? Did he not tell her because he was embarrassed and afraid of her reaction? Did he not tell her because he thought it was none of her business or because his new girlfriend wanted to keep the relationship secret? Could it be that he was swept away by this new relationship and not thinking straight? The hurt feels personal. It feels to Rachel as if her father doesn't care about her and yet the way in which she found out the news – as with so many events in world history – may have been the result of a cock-up rather than a conspiracy.

This goes to the heart of how young people see the world. When bad things happen, surely they can't be accidental? Surely someone must be responsible? Someone must be doing it on purpose!

We talk about her father who became a parent at sixteen. Perhaps he feels that he missed out on his own teenage years? Perhaps we fall for people sometimes and we don't mean to but we do? Perhaps he feels guilty about letting Rachel down? Perhaps this new girlfriend is his way of being angry with Rachel's mother and has no bearing on his feelings about Rachel?

We wonder about these and other possibilities. We wonder whether events might not always be quite as personal as they feel. Bad things might happen which are no one's fault. The upsetting and annoying things that our parents do certainly affect us, but those things might say more about our parents than they say about us.

'I wonder whether they couldn't think what to do about the limousine problem and somehow they forgot about you, Rachel?'

'I doubt that!' she says. 'They knew perfectly well that I was part of it. It was me who planned it all in the beginning!'

'I was wondering whether it was deliberate or whether they just messed up?'

'Why would they mess up?' she says. 'They're supposed to be my friends!'

'They may not have known what to do…?'

She shakes her head in disbelief. 'I can't believe Sarah and Jasmine went along with it!'

'Perhaps Sarah and Jasmine didn't dare say anything?'

She scoffs. 'In that case, you don't know Sarah! She wouldn't be scared of saying something!'

'Did the girls actually have a meeting about it?'

'Doubt it.'

'All I'm saying is that it might not have been deliberate. It might have been an accident…'

'So why hasn't anyone come and spoken to me about it? I mean, how would they feel if it happened to them?'

'Maybe that's why they can't say anything? Maybe they're feeling guilty because they know you're angry and they don't know what to do about it?'

Most young people negotiate their way out of primary narcissism (Freud 1914), no longer believing that the world revolves around them and gradually accepting the fact that they must share power with other people. But when things go badly, when life feels suddenly unfair, young people cast around for someone to blame because that simplifies things. The idea that *no one's* to blame implies that the world may not be quite as persecutory as they imagined and that they themselves may not be quite as important as they imagined. In fact, the world may not be very interested in the ups and downs of one young person's life.

His father has said that Ibra's no son of his. This has hurt Ibra terribly although in public he maintains an air of insouciance.

'Maybe he feels he's losing control of you as you get older and so he's lashing out?'

'It wasn't like that,' says Ibra. 'He was calm. He knew exactly what he was saying.'

'Maybe he's secretly afraid of you getting into some kind of danger?'

Ibra scoffs. 'Maybe he's a complete wanker!'

'Or maybe sometimes he says things to hurt people?'

'Why would he do that?'

'I don't know. Because he's getting old? Because he's afraid that he's wasted his own life? Because he's jealous of you?'

'But if you're a dad you're not supposed to be jealous of your kids. You're supposed to love them!'

'What if you have mixed feelings about them?'

'Then you shouldn't have kids, should you!'

'So would it make you a bad father if you didn't like everything about your kids?'

'Of course!'

'But, Ibra, you've said in the past that you don't like everything about Nissa…'

'That's different,' he says. 'Nissa's my girlfriend. She's not my kid!'

'Why is that different? Maybe it's normal to dislike things about people we love?'

'You're weird!' he says, smiling.

If the cause of our distress is less personal than we supposed, if it's not because our parents or teachers have been deliberately plotting our downfall, then why *do* bad things happen? Who decides? God? Satan? Is there anything we can do to protect ourselves from bad things happening and, if not, why not? Okay, we can understand certain things… 'My dad behaves like that because *his* dad behaved like that… My mum worries about money because her family never had any…' But other things can't be explained so easily. 'Why did my brother get cancer? Why do people kill each other? Why do accidents happen? Why do we have to die? Is everything a cock-up or is everything a conspiracy?'

Kingston has just got the results of some public exams and he's done badly. He says his mother won't mind because she knows that he did his best.

His father died a year ago. I ask what his father would say.

'He'd say it doesn't matter because I can retake them. But I'm gutted all the same,' Kingston says, looking away. 'It's weird. I feel like I'm a nobody. Like I'm pointless. Like I'm trapped.'

I wasn't expecting him to use words like these. We've talked a lot about his father over the last year and I've been at pains to make sure that we talk about other things as well – normal teenage things like friends and enemies and all the funny stuff that happens – because it's important that Kingston doesn't become merely 'that-poor-boy-whose-father-died'. I think that our conversations have made it perfectly clear that Kingston's life is interesting in all sorts of ways that have nothing to do with his father's death. So I wasn't expecting him to use words like 'nobody', 'pointless' and 'trapped' in connection with exam results.

'I know I can retake them,' he says, 'but I'm still completely gutted.'

Normally cheerful and smiling, he looks pale today, avoiding my eye. I think he's trying to talk about something that connects his experience of these exams with his father's death; something about the *finality* of exams and the brute, unshakeable fact that, ultimately, he's on his own and responsible for his own life. Nothing can change the grades he's got: no amount of sympathy, friendship or reassurance. The exams are done. The grades are published. And in that sense he *is* pointless, trapped, a nobody even, unable to control life's fairnesses and unfairnesses.

It's a tough realisation. As the weeks go by, we keep coming back to it, our philosophising mixed in with gossiping and laughing about other things. Sometimes he gets frightened about life's finality, then forgets about all that stuff and talks about football. Weeks later, he gets frightened again. Then forgets again. We keep talking. I make it clear that I have no answers but can help him to bear his panic and fear.

Not having the answers is important because it's easy for counsellors and other professionals supporting young people to attract positive rather than negative transferences. I know that Kingston likes me. He tells his friends I'm cool. It's easy for counsellors to seem like the parents who *do* care, who *do* have time and who *do* understand. Unlike real parents, counsellors don't have to quarrel with young people over bedtimes or coming home drunk or getting homework done on time. Because of the ease with which they can be idealised, counsellors therefore have to develop a capacity to disappoint, to be ordinarily imperfect. They have to make clear their inability to wave magic wands or change a young person's circumstances. They have to be clear that, after the apparent wonders of counselling, life will *still* be unfair, things will *still* go wrong, death will *still* happen. It may be inevitable that young people will idealise their counsellors for a while but, as soon as the time is right, the counsellors have to step off their pedestals.

Things that go wrong in counselling are therefore always therapeutic opportunities. There's an opportunity to step off the pedestal whenever a counsellor misunderstands something and, instead of pretending otherwise, admits as much. There's an opportunity whenever a counsellor is late for an appointment and, instead of blaming the traffic, apologises.

'I'm late. I'm sorry.'

'That's okay. Don't worry.'

'No, it's not okay but it's happened.'

For perfectly good therapeutic reasons, counsellors prefer to see young people at the same time and in the same room every week. Counselling training teaches the importance of consistency and, for young people whose lives have often been chaotic, consistency is vital. So whenever something goes unexpectedly wrong, it's tempting for counsellors to throw up their hands in horror. Typically, someone barges in during a session. Or the normal counselling room has been double-booked. Or someone's left it in a mess. Or a fire alarm interrupts the session. Or time is lost finding an alternative to the double-booked room. I work in schools and, much as I prefer to have the same room every week, there are occasions when this isn't possible. Nor is it always possible to warn young people about these changes.

'I'm afraid your room's not available today because it's needed for an exam and there's nowhere else to do the exam. Did no one tell you?'

The young person is watching. If I throw up my hands in professional horror, cursing under my breath, glaring at the poor messenger and – in all sorts of other ways – indicating my disgust, the message to the young person is that untoward events like these are catastrophic and that all the untoward things happening in a young person's life are also catastrophic therefore. But if I can allow that things *do* go wrong, that they're not ideal but – hey – we'll cope, then the message to young people is that they too can cope. Okay, so sometimes we have to meet in a different room which is untidy and a bit cold and not entirely sound-proofed.

Big deal! We can make this an interesting rather than problematic experience. After all, it's our conversation that matters, not the room in which we have the conversation. This message to young people is important: when things go wrong as they inevitably will go wrong, we won't panic, we won't lash out; we'll make the best of a bad situation, adapting in the same way that a baby must learn to adapt to 'environmental impingements' (Winnicott 1965, 1975).

And things go wrong that are far worse than a mere change of room. I remember supervising counsellors who found out that their entire service was being disbanded in a few months' time. This was devastating news for professionals who had put so much into their service. It was terribly unfair and certainly of no help to any of the distressed young people currently using the service who were about to learn that their open-ended counselling relationships were about to become very time-limited. Six weeks left, then five weeks, then four…

But it was also a therapeutic opportunity – a chance for the young people to experience something going badly wrong which, with the support of their counsellor, they could live through without panicking. With support, they could bear the unfairness of the situation and survive, taking what was useful rather than dwelling on what wasn't, absorbing it as important learning *modelled* by the counsellor's attitude of exasperated but reflective and interested concern. 'This is what life's like,' the counsellor might effectively be saying. 'Things go wrong sometimes and we wish they didn't. We feel strongly about them. Sometimes there are practical things we can do to improve the situation but – whatever happens – we won't be destroyed.'

The fact that things go wrong, that sometimes it's no one's fault and that there's nothing we can do about it, is news to young people struggling to accept that no one is guaranteeing them happiness.

'I shouldn't be feeling like this!' complains Seth. 'I've got my family and all my friends. I've got loads going for me. I should be happy!'

Bad things have been happening in his life recently and he can't understand why. A century ago, he wouldn't have been surprised. He'd have expected school to be harsh and work to be repetitive. He'd have expected life to be dangerous and unfair. He'd have expected close relatives to get ill and die. His view of the world would have been influenced by the socio-economic, educational and medical circumstances of the time.

Nowadays, many young people are thrown whenever something goes wrong and they can make no sense whatsoever of the experience. 'How could my gran possibly be dying? How could my dad possibly have lost his job? When I wanted to succeed and worked so hard, how could I possibly have failed?' Frantically, they seek explanations to make the bad experience go away. It must be a conspiracy of some sort. It must be someone's fault.

We have no right to happiness. We can't earn it or buy it. And yet there's a widespread assumption nowadays that we *should* be happy, and that if we're not, then it must be someone's fault. 'Why is this happening to me? Why have things gone wrong? Why is no one making my life better?' The 'positive thinking' industry has a lot to answer for (Ehrenreich 2009). 'Think positively,' they say, 'and your problems will vanish. Think positively and you'll feel better. Think positively and your dreams will come true. Your cancer might even go away!'

It's complete nonsense. I think we need to remind young people that life *is* short, bad things *do* happen and people *do* die. There are times when I sit with a young person and there's nothing to say, nothing to do. Life sucks.

'Why?' asks Jenna, in tears. 'I don't understand why!'

Her best friend's mother has just been diagnosed with breast cancer. I say that I don't understand either.

'But there must be a reason?' she says, looking to me for an answer.

I have nothing to say. Jenna can be angry with me if she wants. She can certainly be disappointed. But to pretend that her best friend's mother's cancer has developed *for a reason* would be unfair. As young people say, shit happens sometimes and we don't know why it happens. Only when we admit as much can we begin to move on and enjoy all the good things in life. They're only good because they don't last forever.

9

MORALITY AND DEATH

'Why don't you tell the truth? Why d'you only care about yourself? Why go along with what they're doing when you know it's wrong?'

Young people are regularly castigated for their immoral or amoral behaviour, and it's certainly true that they do cheat sometimes, do tell lies sometimes and do involve themselves in all sorts of things that they shouldn't. Sometimes. In fact, they can be as greedy and cowardly as any adult. Yet they can also be brave, self-sacrificing and kind. So where do these very different moral behaviours come from?

Young people certainly wouldn't use words like 'morality', 'moral values' or 'moral behaviours'. Instead, they talk passionately about what's fair and not fair:

'That's not fair!'

'Why isn't it fair?'

'Because it's not!'

It's easier to say what's *not* fair than what *is* fair because what *is* fair is complicated. Usually it involves giving and taking, balancing one person's rights against another person's. More often than not, it involves compromising when young people don't always feel like compromising.

According to Piaget (1932), children begin their lives by learning a simple moral realism, making judgements based on objective facts ('When I hit my sister it makes her cry'), before going on to develop more complex moral ideas based on notions of cooperation and reciprocity. Kohlberg (1958) extends Piaget's work, outlining six stages of moral development as children gradually learn about balancing the rights of the individual ('That's mine!') with those of the group ('We've got to share!'). As they get older, young people continue to explore the complexities of giving and taking, of fairness and unfairness:

'I never get a turn!'

'That's because you always spoil it for other people!'

'But you never give me a chance!'

'Why should we, when you can't be trusted?'

The trouble with outlining 'stages of development' is that the 'stages' always sound as if they follow each other down a neat, linear path, whereas, in fact, young people's development is usually erratic: regressing and then jumping forward, getting stuck and then unstuck, regressing again and jumping forward again... Their eventual ability to recognise and tolerate the existence of other people comes from the security of feeling that they exist and matter themselves without having to fight anyone to prove it. But the security of that feeling comes and goes and with it comes and goes the ability to tolerate other people. At one extreme, I listen to Adam – who'll admit that he's never felt loved in his life – advocating a 'fuck and chuck' approach to relationships with girls. At the other extreme, Laura – whose parents have always doted on her – tells me that her friends are everything to her. 'I'd do anything for them!' she says. Adam and Laura's morality – their ability to bear a world of give and take, cruelty and kindness – is considerably influenced by earlier experiences at the hands of their parents.

But young people's moral perspective, their sense of fairness and unfairness, is also informed by the growing awareness that life doesn't go on forever and that, however saintly they may or may not be, they'll end up dead. Any sense of life's fairness must therefore account for the seeming *unfairness* of painful deaths, of sudden deaths, of good people dying and dying young; it must account for the unfairness (or perhaps for the absolute *fairness*) of everyone dying eventually.

Young people respond to this awareness in different ways. Some will argue simply that 'shit happens!' and that's all there is to know. Others will insist that 'everything happens for a reason'. Still others will claim that a superior being is deciding what we do or don't deserve and is making these decisions based on our earthly performances.

The way we come to think about death has a considerable bearing on the moral perspectives we adopt. If life is made worthless by the certainty of death, for example, then Adam might well conclude that other people's feelings don't matter: you might as well fuck and chuck. But if, on the other hand, life is made precious by the certainty of death, then Laura might conclude that other people's feelings are the *only* things that matter. Adam's self-centredness and Laura's apparent altruism represent a moral compass twitching between extremes. Adam might go on to argue that if nothing matters, if everything is deprived of value because we're all going to die anyway, then other people and their rights are never going to be of any consequence. But since we're born to die, Laura might respond, we might as well devote ourselves to other people in the hope that our lives will acquire some meaning beyond the basely selfish.

Whenever young people are at any sort of moral crossroads with an important decision to make, we often conclude our advice to them by noting ruefully (and irritably) that 'life's too short'. What we imply is that death will get us all in the end so... Why be unkind, Adam? Why be self-sacrificing, Laura? Winnicott (1965) describes children developing a 'capacity for concern' or moral conscience as they start to make up for having hated (as well as loved) their parents. He's vague about how exactly this development occurs, but I would suggest that it develops *alongside* a growing awareness that, because 'life's too short', we simply can't afford to carry on hating and making enemies of everybody. We need other people and they need us.

The prospect of death fills young people with urgency on the one hand ('You might as well get on with it because time is limited') and with despair on the other ('You might as well give up because time is limited'). Some young people ricochet alarmingly between these extremes, but if they can be thought about with the help of another person, then a more nuanced response might emerge to temper Adam's extreme self-centredness or Laura's extreme self-sacrifice.

Fallon says lots and says it quickly. She wants to get on with her life. She has lots of friends. She's involved with everything at school. She works hard. She does well. Yet she's come to see me because she's started to get panic attacks, particularly before exams, and these attacks threaten to undermine all her hard work and revision, she says.

As it happens, her father has cancer...

I sometimes think that taking an exam is like dying. Young people go into a big hall and are finally alone, with no one to encourage, love or console them any longer.

Everything is silent. The big clock ticks. The birds sing outside.

It's frightening because it forces young people to take responsibility for their lives. Either they engage with the process, play the game, start writing and do their best or they don't. And having that choice is shocking: the realisation that they probably *do* have some control over their own lives and really *could* choose to write nothing or scrawl obscenities or tear up the exam paper. It's equally frightening in the run-up to the day when the exam results are announced: 'Is my life about to be ruined? What will become of me? What will my life be worth once I've opened the envelope?' It's like waiting for the letter with the result of the hospital tests: it feels like a matter of life and death.

Of course, not all young people will admit to such panicky thoughts: 'I don't care! Doesn't make any difference to me!' But they do care and it does make a difference. The same fears, the same existential choices apply to meeting ordinary coursework deadlines or getting down to ordinary homework. At these moments, young people inevitably ask themselves, 'Why am I doing this? Who am I doing this for? What difference will it make? What's the point?' These are good, important questions to which there are no easy answers. When you strip life down to these questions, it can certainly feel lonely, as lonely as going into a big examination hall. Many young people work to music, I suspect, because having someone singing in your ear makes the task feel less lonely.

Fallon doesn't want to talk about her father's cancer. When I nudge her in that direction, she clams up and won't talk, her anxiety displaced into panicking about the exams, whereas when we talk about schoolwork, she'll happily tell me all about the different subjects she's studying and what she's learning. She'll recount interesting facts about the Russian Revolution and the cause of tsunamis. She'll delight in describing the many eccentricities of her teachers. But she won't talk about what it feels like to go into that examination hall. No way.

I ask what happens.

'What do you mean?'

'What happens when you go into the exam?'

'You know what happens! We go in and sit down. What d'you *think* happens?'

'I was wondering what it felt like...'

'Horrible,' she says. 'I hate it. I can't think... Can we change the subject now?'

I tell her my theory about exams and dying, making no connection with her father's illness.

She says it's an interesting theory. 'I agree about the choice thing... I hate having to choose! I like it when I know what I've got to do because then I can get on with it and do my best.'

'It's scary when we can't control things, Fallon.'

She agrees and quickly changes the subject. Hers is a morality based on 'making the most of your life', which might be a wholly laudable way of approaching life if it wasn't born of panic. Because of her father's illness, she's only too well aware of death waiting at the end of everything but won't (or can't) look at this. For Fallon, make-the-most-of-your-life becomes a manic, unsustainable flight from anxieties about death, just as it does for other young people also dashing around with things to do, places to go, people to see ('Got to make the most of my life!'), phoning, texting, phoning, texting...

For other young people *not* dashing around, *not* phoning or texting all the time, make-the-most-of-your-life becomes a hedonistic imperative – a perfect reason for carousing all night long, enjoying the moment, fuelled with as much alcohol as possible, avoiding any thoughts about the future. Fallon can't do that. Because she knows that anyone can get cancer at any time, she doesn't waste time carousing but seizes every opportunity to do the things that her father – presumably – can no longer do. She does them before it's too late.

I wonder how much her behaviour also expresses an anxiety about simply *being still*, where being still feels like being invisible and being invisible feels like being dead. Everyone has imagined waking up in the darkness of a coffin with no way of alerting the people above ground to their terrible mistake. The manic activity of some young people seems almost to be a response to the prospect of being unable to move, unheard, trapped in the dark, forgotten about and facing certain death. For those young people still dependent on external recognition to bolster a precarious sense of self (Luxmoore 2008) and anxious therefore about being invisible (see Chapter 5), an obvious response is to make as much noise as possible, constantly moving about, constantly being seen, keeping in touch with friends, never alone and never for one moment forgotten.

If these anxieties provoke an urgency in some young people, others respond to the fact of life being short and death being inescapable by doing nothing at all, staying in bed all morning, moping about the house, postponing anything that needs doing and insisting all the while that 'I can't be bothered!' As a very different strategy from Fallon's perpetual hard work, lethargy works just as well, handing all anxieties about time being short over to *other* people, so that the more lethargic the young person becomes, the more his or her parents (typically) jump about in panic.

'When on earth are you going to get on with your life?' Instead of the young person feeling hopeless, the parents feel hopeless. Instead, *they're* filled with desperation by their son or daughter's behaviour. Joseph (1989) writes about people addicted to despair, for whom there's a masochistic pleasure to be had in their own misery. 'There is a felt need to know and to have the satisfaction of seeing oneself being destroyed,' she writes (p.128), describing clients who project all their aliveness and optimism into a therapist, only to enjoy confounding that therapist's best attempts to infuse them with these same qualities. There are lots of young people who fit this description, thwarting all attempts by well-meaning adults to break the pattern. I remember a colleague getting up reluctantly to go and meet with a particularly morose young person. 'Here we go again!' she sighed. 'More doom and gloom from the tomb!'

Charlie, for example, couldn't be more passive if he tried, his face expressionless, his body utterly still. He says as little as possible and I find myself quickly beginning to count any phrase or sentence from Charlie as a major triumph. I feel like shaking him into action, filling up with energy on his behalf, until I discover that his father died suddenly when he was eight. Once I know this, his behaviour makes better sense as a way of responding to what happened, as a numbness and as a way of living with the knowledge that further deaths are possible. Typically, he responds to my questions with never more than a shrug and a few words as if – whatever the question – his unspoken answer is always the same: 'Why are you asking me? What difference does this make? What difference does *anything* make?'

'How's your week been, Charlie?'

A shrug.

'Did you go out on Friday night?'

'Can't remember...'

'How's your mum?'

No reply.

And so on...

'Getting on with your life' might be a laudable moral position but, for young people, the trouble is that it also means getting on with your death. Charlie's response to death isn't 'fight' (like Fallon's manic activity) or 'flight' (like the hedonistic carousing of some young people) but 'freeze'. He doesn't fight or run away from the enemy: he tries to keep things just as they are, perhaps imagining that, this way, nothing will change.

His freeze protects him from feeling or remembering anything about his father's death. I can't decide whether pushing him to speak about this is what he needs from me (it certainly isn't what he *wants*) or whether making him talk about the very thing he doesn't want to talk about would be a way of punishing him for freezing me out of the conversation.

I decide that it's probably what he needs, although he won't thank me for raising the subject. 'I was thinking about your father, Charlie...'

Immediately he looks up. 'Why?'

'I was thinking that he'd be about thirty-eight if he'd lived...'

'So?'

'I guess it would be weird now, having a dad.'

'Wouldn't know!'

'You've got your mum but, apart from her, you've always had to cope on your own. You've had to deal with school, friends, enemies, new stuff happening... He's never been there.'

'So? Makes no difference to me.'

'Because it's been easy, getting on with your life?'

'Not for me to say!'

'I imagine that he'd be proud…'

No response.

'Proud that you're able to get on with your life and do all the things that you do…'

He looks up. 'Why are you asking?'

'Because I was thinking that, even when a person's dead, they don't stop being important.'

'To be honest, I don't think about him.'

This is as much as he's ever said. A tiny thaw.

I continue, 'You're busy getting on with your life so I imagine he wouldn't expect you to be spending time thinking about him…'

'I don't!'

'I know… So when you do think about him, what do you think?'

'Nothing!'

I decide to change the subject, judging that we've done enough.

But Charlie speaks. 'It was his birthday the other day. We put flowers on his grave.'

He's silent again.

'Where's your dad buried?'

'In the cemetery.'

'What was it like, going to visit the grave?'

A shrug.

'I wonder what you found yourself thinking…'

No reply.

It's often said that 'the behaviour is always a solution to the problem', meaning that however odd, disruptive or self-destructive a young person's behaviour might seem, it's never meaningless. Unconsciously, it solves something for the young person. It distracts from a painful feeling, for example, or it gets other people to back off. Charlie's monosyllabic stillness makes sense: it 'solves' the problem of his father's death by silencing any screaming, panic-stricken feelings Charlie might have. It shuts them up and keeps them shut up.

I say, 'I think the way you keep quiet about things makes sense.'

Momentarily, he looks interested.

'I think it's your way of getting on with your life. It's your way of not thinking about stuff. It makes sense.'

Young people's defences are usually criticised as illogical, antisocial or stupid. But to the young person they seemed like the *only* ways of behaving at that time and in those circumstances: 'He was criticising me so I swore at him... She was flirting with my boyfriend so I hit her... I didn't understand the work so I walked out...' Understanding *why* these unconscious defences made sense at the time frees the young person from feeling that whatever he or she did was necessarily 'bad'. Whatever the rights or wrongs of the behaviour, understanding it as a defence allows the young person to start thinking about it as the product of strong feelings. Not as the product of badness, madness or stupidity. And if the feelings can be consciously thought about and recognised, then the behaviour can become more considered.

Montana doesn't do monosyllabic stillness like Charlie. Instead, she rants, sounding like a five-year-old inside a fifteen-year-old's body. 'Everybody hates me!' she insists at the end of her latest story about life's unfairness.

Telling her that she sounds like a five-year-old wouldn't help. The fact is that we *all* have times when we become five-year-olds again, when the world seems to be against us, when those old, childlike feelings take hold and we no longer know what to say or do for the best. 'Everybody hates me!' simplifies life. It disguises Montana's hating of other people by making her out to be the poor victim, and it disguises her desperate need to be loved. 'If I can't be loved, I'll be hated,' she might be saying, in effect. 'At least that way I'll get noticed!'

At times like these, it's important to remember that she really *is* (temporarily) a five-year-old, albeit a five-year-old with heavy make-up and jauntily displaying lots of cleavage. Reasoning with her won't help; punishing her won't help; sarcasm won't help. Only time will dissolve the wave of despair and helplessness washing over her. In a few hours, five-year-old Montana will be transformed back into a fifteen-year-old Montana.

'Everybody hates me! They're always picking on me! And now other people have started!'

'That must be horrible…'

'It is!'

'I'm really sorry, Montana…'

'So am I! And there's nothing I can do about it!'

'No, I don't suppose there is…'

Taking responsibility for her life (and, by implication, for her death) is frightening (see Chapter 10). Rather than offer lots of practical solutions, I sometimes agree with young people about how frightening and difficult life feels, because most are inclined to move on for themselves once adults have stopped pretending to have the answers. By agreeing that life is hopeless, I'm no longer the powerful adult with all the answers, which makes it harder for her to remain the helpless child with none of the answers. She may well now counter my apparent defeatism by suggesting to me a perfectly sensible way of changing the situation herself.

'I'm going find out who started the rumour,' she says. 'I'm going to ask Eloise because the chances are it was her...'

I say nothing.

'When I find out, I'll go mad! I'll kill whoever it was! I mean, how would they like it if someone started saying stuff about them?'

Still I say nothing.

'What goes around comes around! When I find out, I'm going to spread loads of shit about the person and see how they like it!'

'[O]ur sense of ourselves as moral creatures is organised around the question of betrayal,' writes Phillips (2012, p.14). Montana certainly feels betrayed by her peers yet, however immoral other people's betrayal may appear to be, it's a necessary process by which we're able to move on and grow, argues Phillips: '...without betrayal there can be no development' (p.14). The experience of betrayal allows Montana and her peers to change and to keep changing.

Like so many young people, Montana professes to believe in an eye for an eye, a life for a life. I think she does this because, in the world of magical, five-year-old thinking, good people live forever and bad people die – 'Because that's fair!' For a fifteen-year-old, the unfairness of good people dying (and sometimes dying young) makes little moral sense; it feels like a betrayal when bad people are forgiven their crimes and are able to carry on living. The apparent unfairness of this takes a lot of getting used to. 'It's so random!' she might say, echoing Adam's mechanistic fuck-and-chuck philosophy. Yet at times Montana might also sympathise with Laura's idea that relationships give life meaning: we might all be going to die one day but we can care for each other in the meantime, accepting and forgiving each other's faults. We can move on and grow, constantly reinterpreting ourselves.

'Don't they realise what it's like when they make up rumours about other people? Why can't they leave people alone? Haven't they got anything better to do?'

Her enemies have left her feeling isolated. Like other young people, she's frightened of being alone and, at the moment, not having friends sounds like being very alone: it sounds like being dead. But if someone were to care – *really* care – then that would make things less frightening. For this reason, young people are extremely interested in the authenticity of people who *say* they care.

Looking at me quizzically, Jamie asks, 'Do you get paid for this?'

I nod.

'How much?'

I say it's my job.

'What? Listening to people all day?'

I say yes. 'Why do you ask?'

'No reason,' he says. 'I was just thinking that it must get boring.'

'It's never boring,' I say truthfully. 'It's a privilege.'

'But do you actually *like* doing it?'

I think he's wrestling with the old therapy-as-prostitution issue… 'If it's your job and you're being paid to do it, then you obviously don't *really* care or you'd do it for free.'

I tell him that I do it because people matter and people need help from time to time.

'But it's not a normal job, is it!'

'Not a normal job for a man?'

'No, I mean it's not a *normal* type of job. You don't get loads of people wanting to be counsellors!'

Something's nagging away at him that he can't quite put into words. I think he's really asking, 'What are your motives? You act as if you care, but do you really? Why do this if not for the money?'

I remind him that lots of people are paid to do jobs that involve caring for other people. Jobs like youth work, teaching, nursing, social work...

'Yeah, but talking to a counsellor and telling a counsellor all your secrets, that's different!'

'More like talking to a parent?'

He looks confused.

'Maybe parents should get paid, Jamie?'

'No way!' he says. 'It's their job!'

'Being a parent?'

'Yeah! Well, not a job exactly but it's what they've got to do!'

'So why do they do it if they're not being paid?'

'I don't know,' he laughs. 'Haven't a clue!'

'Why *do* people care about each other, Jamie?'

'I don't know!' he says. 'You tell me. Why?'

I say it's a good question and he seems pleased. After all, why *do* we care about each other? Are we just propagating and protecting the species or is there something more? And if there's more – if love isn't mercenary and self-serving – then why bother loving other people when we're going to die and they're going to die as well? Does death make everything pointless? Or does love give everything a point? Is love more important than money?

Jamie's sense of what's morally worth doing will consolidate itself over time. But, interestingly, something in our conversation about people caring for each other has reminded him of his grandfather who died in a hospice.

'That's a job I couldn't do,' he says. 'No way! Looking after dying people… I wouldn't do that, not for any money! People who do that must be…'

'Saints?'

'Yeah!'

Slowly he's puzzling it out. Any young person's moral perspective emerges from personal experience rather than from exposure to abstract philosophical ideas or from listening to the well-meaning exhortations of adults. School assemblies are often intended to instil in young people moral values such as hard work, public spiritedness and respect for those less fortunate than ourselves. Yet, according to Coleman (2011), research demonstrates the ineffectiveness of cognitive approaches designed to speed up young people's moral reasoning ('And so you see, boys and girls…'). I would add that moralising school assemblies are also ineffective because they avoid the subject of death, and death crucially informs our moral reasoning. There's an unfortunate assumption in schools that death is a subject best left to priests and pastors or (better still) avoided altogether in case anyone gets upset or in case thinking about death undermines the school rhetoric about investing in all those exciting futures.

Unless young people are encouraged to talk about death and dying, their moral development remains shallow and defensive. The Association for Death Education and Counselling in the USA has tried to promote in schools a more open approach to the subject of death, despite criticism from some quarters that talking about death might make young people want to kill themselves! Pacholski (1991) writes that 'Death education is worthy of our continued study and teaching because it is a supremely moral subject… Death education enables a person to formulate essential moral judgments...' (p.201). The prospect of death not only informs our moral outlook but profoundly affects our willingness to take responsibility for our own lives.

10

THE PROBLEM OF PERSONAL RESPONSIBILITY

'I don't give a shit!' says Deon. 'This school can fuck itself! They can't make me do anything I don't want to do!'

Although he wouldn't use the phrase, he's come up against the notion of personal responsibility and doesn't like it. He's about to be excluded whether he likes it or not but he can still make things worse: it's up to him. In his latest quarrel with the teachers, he really *does* have a choice and that's scary because, although his teachers care about him, he'll leave school before long and all of this will be of no consequence. In a few years, Deon will be forgotten. I think he's beginning to sense what Yalom (1980) calls the 'cosmic indifference' of the world and his response is a kind of tit-for-tat: if you don't care about me, then I won't care about you. For the time being, he's playing the role of Deon the Supreme Ruler, defying the authorities and fighting against the odds (see Chapter 3). But this latest quarrel isn't really about school; it's about the point of anything, about the point of being alive and about the problem of having to take responsibility for our lives because, ultimately, we're on our own.

There's an assumption in psychotherapy that the way we see the world is determined by our past. There's certainly plenty of truth in this, but the prospect of the future affects us just as powerfully. Because it's often frightening to look into the future, we regress or digress – anything to avoid looking. In a sense, the future is finite whereas the past goes on forever. With the past, we can be endlessly looking back, revisiting and reconstructing our autobiographical narratives, whereas, with the future, we might fantasise about the lives we'll go on to lead but we know that the end of the story will always be the same.

Faced with the inevitability of our death, Yalom (1980) describes two basic kinds of denial: one is the belief that *I am inviolable* (the equivalent of Deon's 'They can't make me do anything I don't want to do!') and the other is the belief that *I will be rescued.*

'Can't you do something?' he asks me, softening. 'Can't you speak to them?'

He's sworn at a teacher very publicly, and so asking me to intercede on his behalf – to rescue him, in effect – will make no difference. He's done what he's done and he'll be punished, however much the teachers may like him or sympathise with the difficulties of his life. The brutality of this may surprise him. Freud (1911) describes how, as we grow up, the self-indulgent 'pleasure principle' is eventually curbed by the development of the 'reality principle', teaching us to tolerate frustration and the fact that the world isn't ours to do with as we wish. Until now, Deon may have been indulged by parents more interested in fighting each other than in providing consistent boundaries for their son. Until now, he may never have come up against the ultimate indifference of the world, meting out its justice regardless of how special he believes himself to be.

I am inviolable... I will be rescued... Young people oscillate between these two ways of defending themselves against the anxiety provoked in them by an awareness of death. They're rude and grandiose one minute, desperate and beseeching the next. They're heroic warriors needing no one and then vulnerable puppies, begging to be looked after. 'Perhaps my counsellor will rescue me...'

'Can't you do something? Can't you speak to them?'

'They'll make their decision,' I say. 'That's what they do. That's what they have to do.'

'But what's the point of that?'

'What do you mean?'

'What's the point of you being the counsellor if you can't do anything?'

'I can help in some ways,' I say, 'but when something like this happens, the school makes its own decision. You'll almost certainly get excluded.'

'I know that,' he says, 'and that's the whole problem because my dad'll *kill* me! I promised him I wouldn't get into any more trouble after last time.'

'So he'll be disappointed...'

'Disappointed? He'll go mad! Are you sure there's nothing you can do? They take notice of you!'

I don't say anything.

'Anyway,' he says, changing tactics, 'I don't give a shit. If my dad kicks me out, Baker says I can sleep on his floor, so it makes no difference to me!'

He's struggling, really struggling, and he's covering his fear with this bombastic stuff. Yet the fear won't go away. His actions have consequences. He knew perfectly well that he shouldn't swear, but he did, challenging the world, risking the consequences. Now he veers between free will and determinism, between Deon the Supreme Ruler and

Deon the Helpless Wretch, between Deon the Bully and Deon the Victim. Like all young people, he must learn to steer a course between these extremes – powerful in some ways, powerless in others – always negotiating with the existential gods.

To say that he's discovered personal responsibility isn't quite true. I think that, like all young people, he's always sensed *unconsciously* that he's responsible for his own actions but he's never allowed that thought to become conscious. His teachers and parents will have berated him, insisting, 'You've got to take responsibility! It's up to you! No one's going to do it for you!' but he's never really *heard* them until now. He'll have convinced himself that some great rescuer would come, some wonderful mother figure to gather him up, soothe his furrowed brow and make everything all right. When this hasn't happened, he's interpreted it as a personal slight ('No one cares about me!') and *hated* whoever seemed to be letting him down so deliberately.

'They know I lose my temper easily and so they *deliberately* wind me up!'

It's a word young people use a lot: 'They *deliberately* picked on me... She was *deliberately* doing it... He *deliberately* refused...' The idea of things being 'deliberate' is philosophically interesting for young people because they're interested in their own capacity to be deliberate, to make choices, to have power, including power over other people.

'I didn't mean to swear! It wasn't deliberate. It just came out.'

'Are you saying it's hard to control yourself, Deon?'

'No, obviously I can control myself! It's just that stuff comes out sometimes!'

'And you lose control...'

'Look, I didn't mean to swear,' he says.

'I didn't mean to do it... I didn't do it deliberately... Don't blame me... It wasn't my fault...' The ideas of 'blame' and 'fault' are also preoccupations for young people and also words they use a lot. Who was to blame? Whose fault was it? Their initial assumption is that blame can be clearly apportioned. And at times they're right – it can – but often the blame or fault is shared and that takes some getting used to: I was partly in control and partly not; partly to blame and partly not.

'I know you said you were being wound up, Deon, but what if both of you were involved? What if the teacher was annoying you and you were annoying the teacher?'

'I suppose...' he says. 'But then I shouldn't get into trouble, should I, because it was his fault as well!'

'That might be true and that's the hard bit.'

'What do you mean?'

'In a school,' I say, 'the school always wins. You swore so you get excluded. The teacher might have been annoying you, but that's the system.'

'So that's completely unfair!'

Whenever young people are railing at the injustice of some particular system, I find myself arguing that you have to beat the system on its own terms before you can change it. There's no point sitting in the bar claiming that exams are stupid and meaningless, for example, if you've failed yours. Your friends will pretend to agree but, privately, they'll be thinking 'Well, he would say that, wouldn't he!' But if you've done well in your exams and *then* argue that they're meaningless, people will take you seriously and then you're in a more powerful position to change the system.

'It might be unfair, but that's the system. We have to play by the rules until we can change them. That's not easy.

It's frustrating sometimes but it's the same with all rules. It's quite scary when you think about it.'

I think it helps young people to accept personal responsibility when adults acknowledge that the experience of doing so isn't easy. Reminding young people that they have freedom, that it's up to them and that nothing's stopping them making changes in their lives, is only telling them what they already know. It doesn't help them to get unstuck. The reason they stay stuck is because freedom and responsibility are scary: *life* is scary and, as generations of young people have reminded their parents, 'I didn't ask to be born!' In Sartre's (1943) phrase, we're 'condemned to be free', and it helps when someone acknowledges the paradox of that. Young people may still mutter darkly about the unfairness of all this but, often, they go away and come back not with consternation and despair but with new resolve, as if acknowledging the scariness has somehow freed them to get on and take more responsibility for their lives, rather than sit around waiting to be rescued.

But Deon hasn't quite reached this point. 'If that's the system,' he says, 'then why can't they make an exception? What difference would it make if they let me off? Just once? I'll be good, I promise!'

Finally, we get to the heart of it, to the Faustian fantasy with which he's been toying but only now daring to voice: 'Why can't they make an exception for me?' or, put differently, 'Why do I have to be like everyone else, subject to the same constraints as everyone else? Why can't I be treated differently?' and, by extension, 'Just because the Big Authority Figure decrees that everyone has to die, why can't I be immortal? Why can't death make an exception for me?'

Yalom (1980) describes a series of apparently unrelated behaviours, all of which are associated with a belief in 'the ultimate rescuer', that person who'll come along and pluck us from the crowd, making an exception for us. These behaviours include 'self-effacement, fear of withdrawal of love, passivity, dependency, self-immolation, refusal to accept adulthood, and depression at the collapse of the belief system' (p.134). In holding on to our misery (Deon the Helpless Wretch), we hold on to the fantasy that someone somewhere will rescue us from it. In letting go of that fantasy, we start to think about what we can do to help ourselves.

With adult freedoms come adult understandings that all of this must one day end, that immortality won't be possible: death won't make an exception. Young people's behaviour is sometimes best understood as a grieving for this realisation. Deon is going through a kind of bereavement as the simplicities of childhood are replaced by adult realities where 'No one can do it for you! You have to do it for yourself! No one's going to come along and rescue you!' Like anyone, he responds to the loss of his rescue fantasy with denial ('They can't make me do anything!'), anger ('This school can fuck itself!'), bargaining ('Can't they make an exception? I'll be good!') and depression – behaviours in no particular order but jumbled up and repeating themselves.

For now, he slumps in his chair, miserable. I resist the temptation to rescue him with advice about what he should do next. He knows perfectly well. *What to do next* isn't the problem. The problem is 'Why do I have to do it?' and 'Why can't anyone do it for me?'

'It's tough,' I repeat. 'Tough and annoying and scary...'

He says nothing. In half an hour, he'll meet with the headteacher who'll exclude him from school for one day for swearing. Deon will then have a choice about whether to swear at the headteacher and make the situation worse, arguing over the details of what originally happened and whose fault it was, or accept that this is a fight he can't win and take his punishment.

I say all of this to him.

'But it's so unfair…!'

I say yes, it *does* feel like that sometimes.

He looks up, 'Are you sure there's nothing…?'

But he knows already. He gets up and leaves with a melodramatic sigh, as if still half expecting me to bail him out, and I'm reminded of the wedding guest in 'The Rime of the Ancient Mariner' who, at the end of everything:

> …went like one that hath been stunned,
> And is of sense forlorn:
> A sadder and a wiser man,
> He rose the morrow morn.
>
> (Coleridge in Beer 1986, p.189)

It probably takes us a lifetime to become wiser men and women, accepting that we won't be rescued and that immortality won't be possible. Deon is only just beginning. I imagine meeting him in ten years' time. We'll be in a supermarket or petrol station and I'll hear a voice behind.

'Remember me?'

I'll look round and I won't remember: partly because he'll look so different from the fifteen-year-old boy I knew all those years ago whose photo was once pinned to the staff noticeboard, partly because he'll have been replaced in my memory by lots of other fifteen-year-old boys and partly because he won't think to remind me of his name.

'I'm the one who used to get into all the trouble!' he'll say. 'Remember? I was a nightmare. All the teachers hated me. I used to come and see you…'

I'll probably lie. 'Of course! How are you?'

He'll introduce me to his distracted girlfriend, waiting a few yards away with their baby daughter. He'll tell me that he's sorted himself out now, that he's working for a firm of builders and doing really well.

I'll say how pleased I am.

He'll joke again about the bad old days at school and, together, we'll laugh.

'They've probably still got my photo up in the staffroom!' he'll say. 'Bet they have! Bet they still go on about me, don't they?'

I won't have the heart to tell him the truth.

REFERENCES

Adams, K. (2010) *Unseen Worlds: Looking through the Lens of Childhood.* London: Jessica Kingsley Publishers.

Barnes, J. (2008) *Nothing to Be Frightened of.* London: Jonathan Cape.

Becker, E. (1973) *The Denial of Death.* New York, NY: The Free Press.

Blos, P. (1962) *On Adolescence: A Psychoanalytic Interpretation.* New York, NY: The Free Press.

Bollas, C. (1999) *The Mystery of Things.* London: Routledge.

Bowlby, J. (1969, 1973, 1980) *Attachment and Loss.* Volumes 1, 2 and 3. London: Hogarth Press.

Coleman, J.C. (2011) *The Nature of Adolescence.* Hove: Routledge.

Coleridge, S.T. (1986) 'The Rime of the Ancient Mariner.' In J. Beer (ed.) *Poems.* London: J.M. Dent.

Davies, J. (2012) *The Importance of Suffering: The Value and Meaning of Emotional Discontent.* London: Routledge.

Diamond, J. (1998) *C: Because Cowards Get Cancer Too.* London: Vermilion.

Ehrenreich, B. (2009) *Smile or Die: How Positive Thinking Fooled America and the World.* London: Granta Publications.

Erikson, E.H. (1950) *Childhood and Society.* London: Vintage Books.

Forster, E.M. (1910, 1992) *Howard's End.* Everyman Library. London: David Campbell Publishers.

Frankel, R. (1998) *The Adolescent Psyche: Jungian and Winnicottian Perspectives.* London: Routledge.

Frayn, M. (2010) *My Father's Fortune: A Life.* London: Faber.

Freud, S. (1911) *Formulations on the Two Principles of Mental Functioning.* Standard Edition. Volume 12. London: Hogarth Press.

Freud, S. (1914) *On Narcissism.* Standard Edition. Volume 14. London: Hogarth Press.

Freud, S. (1920) *Beyond the Pleasure Principle*. Standard Edition. Volume 18. London: Hogarth Press.

Freud, S. (1923) *The Ego and the Id*. Standard Edition. Volume 19. London: Hogarth Press.

Fromm, E. (1963) *The Art of Loving*. New York, NY: Bantam Books.

Gersie, A. (1991) *Storymaking in Bereavement*. London: Jessica Kingsley Publishers.

Heidegger, M. (1962) *Being and Time*. Oxford: Blackwell Publishing.

Hobson, R.E. (1985) *Forms of Feeling: The Heart of Psychotherapy*. London: Routledge.

Joseph, B. (1989) 'Addiction to Near Death.' In E. Bott Spillius and M. Feldman (eds) *Psychic Equilibrium and Psychic Change: Selected Papers of Betty Joseph*. London: Routledge.

Klein, M. (1957) *Envy and Gratitude: A Study of Unconscious Sources*. London: Tavistock Publications.

Klein, M. (1975) 'A Contribution to the Psychogenesis of Manic-Depressive States.' In *Collected Works of Melanie Klein*. Volume 1. London: Hogarth Press and Institute of Psychoanalysis. (Original work published 1935.)

Knox, J. (2011) *Self-Agency in Psychotherapy: Attachment, Autonomy and Intimacy*. New York, NY, and London: W.W. Norton & Company.

Kohlberg, L. (1958) 'The Development of Modes of Thinking and Choices in Years 10 to 16.' PhD Dissertation. Chicago, IL: University of Chicago.

Kohut, H. (1971) *The Analysis of the Self: A Systematic Approach to the Psychoanalytic Treatment of Narcissistic Personality Disorders*. New York, NY: International Universities Press.

Kubler-Ross, E. (1969) *On Death and Dying*. New York, NY: Simon & Schuster.

Langs, R. (1997) *Death Anxiety and Clinical Practice*. London: Karnac Books.

Larkin, P. (2003) *Collected Poems*. Australia: The Marvell Press and London: Faber and Faber.

Lifton, R. (1974) 'The Sense of Immortality: On Death and the Continuity of Life.' In R. Lifton and E. Olson (eds) *Explorations of Psychohistory*. New York, NY: Simon & Schuster.

Luxmoore, N. (2000) *Listening to Young People in School, Youth Work and Counselling*. London: Jessica Kingsley Publishers.

Luxmoore, N. (2002) 'Can We Do Something? Young People Using Action Methods to Support Each Other in School.' In A. Bannister and A. Huntington (eds) *Communicating with Children and Adolescents*. London: Jessica Kingsley Publishers.

Luxmoore, N. (2006) *Working with Anger and Young People*. London: Jessica Kingsley Publishers.

Luxmoore, N. (2008) *Feeling like Crap: Young People and the Meaning of Self-Esteem.* London: Jessica Kingsley Publishers.

Luxmoore, N. (2010) *Young People in Love and in Hate.* London: Jessica Kingsley Publishers.

Luxmoore, N. (2011) *Young People and the Curse of Ordinariness.* London: Jessica Kingsley Publishers.

Mann, T. (1912, 1973) *Death in Venice.* London: Penguin Books.

May, R. (1975) *The Courage to Create.* New York, NY: W.W. Norton & Co.

Meltzer, D. and Harris Williams, M. (1988) *The Apprehension of Beauty: The Role of Aesthetic Conflict in Development, Art and Violence.* Perthshire: Clunie Press.

Mountford, B. (2011) *Christian Atheist: Belonging without Believing.* Alresford: John Hunt Publishing.

Orgler, H. (1975) *Alfred Adler, the Man and his Work.* London: Sidgewick & Jackson.

Pacholski, R.A. (1991) 'The Effectiveness of Death Education.' In J.D. Morgan (ed.) *Young People and Death.* Philadelphia, PA: The Charles Press.

Phillips, A. (2010) *On Balance.* London: Hamish Hamilton.

Phillips, A. (2012) 'Judas' Gift.' *London Review of Books 34*, 1.

Piaget, J. (1932) *The Moral Judgement of the Child.* London: Routledge and Kegan Paul.

Reiner, R. (1986) *Stand by Me.* USA: Columbia Pictures.

Russell, B. (1925) *What I Believe.* London: Kegan Paul.

Sartre, J.P. (1943) *Being and Nothingness.* Paris: Editions Gallimard.

Schopenhauer, A. (1969) *The World as Will and Representation.* Volume 2. New York, NY: Dover Publications.

Schopenhauer, A. (1970) *Essays and Aphorisms.* London: Penguin Books.

Storr, A. (1972) *The Dynamics of Creation.* London: Secker & Warberg.

Tillich, P. (1952) *The Courage to Be.* New Haven, CT: Yale University Press.

Weldon, E. (1988) *Mother, Madonna, Whore: The Idealization and Denigration of Motherhood.* New York, NY: The Guilford Press.

Winnicott, D.W. (1964) *The Child, the Family and the Outside World.* London: Tavistock Publications.

Winnicott, D.W. (1965) *The Maturational Processes and the Facilitating Environment.* London: Hogarth Press.

Winnicott, D.W. (1971) *Playing and Reality.* London: Routledge.

Winnicott, D.W. (1975) *Through Paediatrics to Psychoanalysis.* London: Karnac Books.

Winnicott, D.W. (1989) 'Fear of Breakdown.' In C. Winnicott, R. Shepherd and M. Davis (eds) *Psycho-Analytic Explorations.* London: Karnac Books.

Yalom, I.D. (1980) *Existential Psychotherapy*. New York, NY: Basic Books.

Yalom, I.D. (2008) *Staring at the Sun: Overcoming the Dread of Death.* London: Piatkus Books.

Yeats, W.B. (1999) 'Sailing to Byzantium' from *The Tower*. London: Penguin Books.

INDEX

Printed in Great Britain
by Amazon